Bloom's Literary Guide

DUBLIN

LONDON

NEW YORK

PARIS

ROME

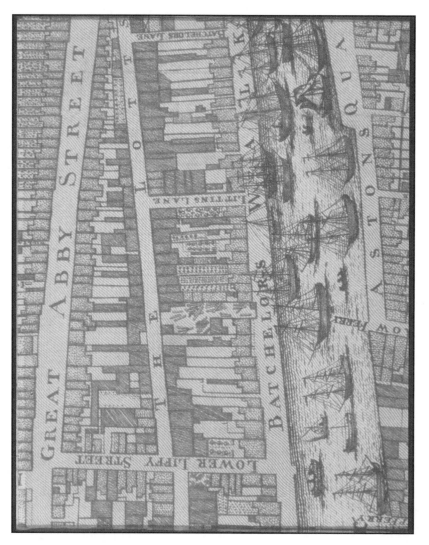

Map of Dublin on 10 Punt Note

Bloom's Literary Guide to

DUBLIN

John Tomedi

Introduction by
Harold Bloom

Checkmark Books®
An imprint of Infobase Publishing
DCM 8213 1186

Bloom's Literary Guide to Dublin

Copyright © 2007 by Infobase Publishing
Introduction copyright © 2007 by Harold Bloom

Checkmark Books
An imprint of Infobase Publishing
132 West 31st Street
New York NY 10001

Library of Congress Cataloging-in-Publication Data

Tomedi, John.
  Dublin / John Tomedi.
    p. cm. — (Bloom's literary guide)
  Includes bibliographical references and index.
  ISBN 0-7910-9376-X (pbk.)
  1. Literary landmarks—Ireland—Dublin. 2. English literature—Irish authors—History and criticism. 3. Authors, Irish—Homes and haunts—Ireland—Dublin. 4. Dublin (Ireland)—Intellectual life. 5. Dublin (Ireland)—In literature. I. Title. II. Series.
  PR110.D79T66 2007
  820.9'941835—dc22   2007013971

Checkmark Books are available at special discounts when purchased in bulk quantities for businesses, associations, institutions, or sales promotions. Please call our Special Sales Department in New York at (212) 967-8800 or (800) 322-8755.

You can find Facts On File on the World Wide Web at
http://www.factsonfile.com

Series and cover design by Takeshi Takahashi

Printed in the United States of America

Bang EJB 10 9 8 7 6 5 4 3 2 1

This book is printed on acid-free paper.

TABLE OF CONTENTS ⬤

HAROLD **BLOOM**

Cities of the Mind

It could be argued that the ancestral city for the Western literary imagination is neither Athens nor Jerusalem, but ancient Alexandria, where Hellenism and Hebraism fused and were harvested. All Western writers of authentic aesthetic eminence are Alexandrians, whether they know it or not. Proust and Joyce, Flaubert and Goethe, Shakespeare and Dante rather uneasily share in that eclectic heritage. From the mid third century before the Common Era through the mid third century after, Alexandria was the city of the spirit and mind and where Plato and Moses did not reconcile (which would be impossible) but abrasively stimulated a new kind of sensibility that we have learned to call Modernism, now twenty-six centuries old. The first Modernist was the poet Callimachus, who said that a long poem was a long evil, and together with his colleagues were approvingly named as *neoteroi* (modernists) by Aristarchus, the earliest literary critic to attempt making a secular canon. Dr. Samuel Johnson, Boileau, Sainte-Beuve, Lessing, Coleridge, I.A. Richards, Empson, and Kenneth Burke are descendants of Aristarchus.

F.E. Peters, in his lucid *The Harvest of Hellenism*, summarizes the achievement of Hellenistic Alexandria by an impressive cat-alog: "Gnosticism, the university, the catechetical school, pas-toral poetry, monasticism, the romance, grammar, lexicography, city planning, theology, canon law, heresy and scholasticism." I don't know why Peters omitted neo-Platonism, inaugurated by Plotinius, and I myself already have added literary criticism, and further would list the library. Alexandria has now exiled its Greeks, Jews, and mostly everyone else not an Arab, and so it is no longer the city of the mind, and of the poetic tradition that went the long span from Callimachus to Cavafy. Yet we cannot arrive at a true appreciation of literary places unless we begin with Alexandria. I recommend the novelist E.M. Forster's guide to the city, which deeply ponders its cultural significance.

We are all Alexandrians, as even Dante was, since he depended upon Hellenistic Neo-Platonic interpretations of Homer, whose poetry he had never read. Virgil, Dante's guide, was Hellenistic in culture, and followed Theocritus in pastoral and Alexandrian imitations of Homer in epic. But though our literary culture remains Alexandrian (consider all our ongoing myths of Modernism), we follow St. Augustine in seeing Jerusalem as the City of God, of King David and his martyred descendant Jesus of Nazareth. Our universities, inescapably Alexandrian in their pragmatic eclecticism, nevertheless con-tinue to exalt the Athens of Socrates, Plato, and Aristotle as the city of cognition and of (supposed) democracy. The actual Peri-clean Athens was a slave-owning oligarchy and plutocracy, which still prevails in much of the world, be it Saudia Arabia or many of the Americas. Literary Athens, in its Golden Age, built on Homer and produced the only Western drama that can chal-lenge Shakespeare: Aeschylus, Euripides, Sophocles, and the divine Aristophanes (I follow Heinrich Heine who observed that: "There is a God and his name is Aristophanes").

Athens now slumbers except for Olympic games and tourism, while Jerusalem is all too lively as the center of Israeli-Arab contention. Alas, their literary glories have waned, but so have those of Rome, where Virgil and even the Florentine

Dante are little read or emulated. Cities of the mind are still represented by Paris and London, both perhaps at this moment in cognitive decline. The international language is now American English, and New York City is therefore the literary place-of-places. That, of necessity, has mixed consequences, but those sharpen my renewed comparison to ancient Alexandria, which mingled inventiveness with high decadence, at the end of an age. Alexandria was consciously belated and so are we, despite our paradoxical ecstasy of the new.

2

Is a literary place, by pragmatic definition, a city? Pastoral, like all other literary forms, was an urban invention. The Hebrew Bible, redacted in Babylonian exile, has as its core in Genesis, Exodus, and Numbers, the Yahwist's narrative composed at Solomon's highly sophisticated court in Jerusalem. We cannot locate the inception of what became *Iliad* and *Odyssey*, but the Greece they taught centered at Athens and Thebes. Florence exiled Dante and Cavalcanti, yet shared all further vernacular literary development with Rome and Milan. If Montaigne tended to isolate himself from embattled Paris, he knew his readers remained there. Elizabethan-Jacobean literature is virtually all fixated upon London, and centers upon Shakespeare's Globe Theater. If the American Renaissance emanates out of the Concord of Emerson, Thoreau, Hawthorne, it is equally at home in the New York City of Whitman, Melville, and the burgeoning James family. Though Faulkner kept, as much as he could, to Oxford, Mississippi, and Wallace Stevens to Hartford, if I had to nominate the ultimate classic of the United States in the twentieth century, unhesitatingly I would choose the poetry of Hart Crane, Whitman's legitimate heir as the bard of New York City. Kenneth Burke, whenever I saw him from 1975 on, would assure me again that Whitman's "Crossing Brooklyn Ferry" and Hart Crane's *The Bridge* were the two greatest American poems.

Our best living novelists—Philip Roth, Pynchon, DeLillo—

have become inseparable from the ethos of New York City. Only the elusive Cormac McCarthy, seer of *Blood Meridian*, keeps far away from the city-of-cities, which has displaced London and Paris as the world's imaginative capital.

3

However solitary a major writer is by vocation, he or she tends to find a closest friend in a contemporary literary artist. Perhaps rivals attract: Shakespeare and Ben Jonson, Byron and Shelley, Hawthorne and Melville, Hemingway and Scott Fitzgerald, Eliot and Pound, Hart Crane and Allen Tate are just a few pairings, to stay within Anglo-American tradition. Yet the tendency is everywhere: Goethe and Schiller, Wordsworth and Coleridge, Swift and Pope, Tolstoy and Chekhov, Henry James and Edith Wharton, and many more, too numerous to list. The locales waver: Hemingway and Fitzgerald in Paris, Byron and Shelley in Italian exile together, Eliot and Pound in London. There are giant exceptions: Cervantes, Milton, Victor Hugo, Emily Dickinson, Joyce and Beckett (though only after their early association).

Cities are the essential requisite for literary relationships, including those dominated by a father-figure, the London assemblage of the Sons of Ben Jonson: Carew, Lovelace, Herrick, Suckling, Randoph and many more, or Dr. Samuel Johnson and his club of Boswell, Goldsmith, Burke, among others, or Mallarmé and his disciples, including Valéry, who was to surpass his master. Modernist London always calls up Bloomsbury, with Virginia Woolf as its luminous figure, the ornament of a group that in its own idiosyncratic mode saw E.M. Forster as its patriarch.

Even in the age of the computer screen, proximity is essential for literary fellowship. But so far I have considered the city as literary place only in regard to writers. As subject, indeed as *the given* of literature, the city is a larger matter. The movement from garden to city as literary focus is powerfully clear in the Hebrew Bible, when Yahweh moves his abode from Mount

Sinai to Mount Zion, and thus to Solomon's Temple. As the mountain of the Covenant, Sinai stands at the origin, but surprisingly Ezekiel (28:13 following) locates "Eden, the garden of God" as a plateau on Zion, both cosmological mountain and paradise. When Yahweh takes up residence in the Temple, his Eden is close by, yet nevertheless the transition from garden to city has been accomplished. This is the Holy City, but to the literary imagination all the great cities are sacred: Paris, London, Dublin, Petersburg, Rome, and New York are also sanctified, whatever suffering and inequity transpire in them.

4

In the United States the national capital, Washington, D.C., is scarcely a city of the mind, not only when contrasted to New York City, but also to Boston, Chicago, San Francisco. Paris, London, and Rome are at once capitals and literary centers, but Washington, D.C. has harbored few major American writers and has provided subjects only for political novelists, like Henry Adams and Gore Vidal. The Great American Novel perpetually remains to be written, despite such earlier splendors as *The Scarlet Letter*, *Moby-Dick*, *Huckleberry Finn*, and *The Portrait of a Lady*, and a handful of later masterpieces from *As I Lay Dying* and *The Sound and the Fury*, *The Sun Also Rises* and *The Great Gatsby*, on to *Gravity's Rainbow*, *Sabbath's Theater*, *Underworld*, and *Blood Meridian*. I rather doubt that it will take Washington, D.C. as subject, or be composed by an inhabitant thereof.

The industrialization of the great cities in the nineteenth century gave us the novels of Victor Hugo, Dickens, Zola which produced a realism totally phantasmagoric, now probably no longer available to us. Computer urbanism does not seem likely to stimulate imaginative literature. Visual overdetermination overwhelms the inward eye and abandons us to narrative or the formal splendors of poetry and drama. There is something hauntingly elegiac about fresh evocations of literary places, here and now in the early years of the twenty-first century.

HAROLD **BLOOM**

Introduction

The greatest Anglo-Irish writers are Jonathan Swift, William Butler Yeats, James Joyce, and Samuel Beckett. But such a judgment needs to allow literary space for Oscar Wilde and George Bernard Shaw, and for the post-Yeatsian tradition in poetry that centers upon Seamus Heaney. Even this extension neglects the truth that English drama, after Shakespeare, comes alive only in Anglo-Irish writers: Congreve, Sheridan, Goldsmith are part of a cavalcade that proceeds through Shaw and Wilde, Synge and O'Casey, before its apotheosis in Beckett.

Dublin is a point of origin for almost all the figures I have cited, and for Edmund Burke, critic and orator, yet Dublin was not the center of literary activity for most of them. London (or Paris, in Beckett's instance) prevails over Dublin as the marketplace of ideas and of a reading public. Yeats alternated between the Irish countryside and Dublin, where he presided over the Abbey Theater, and Joyce exiled himself to Trieste, Zurich, and Paris. Yeats, the major Anglo-Irish poet, cannot be called the poet-dramatist of Dublin. Joyce, who fled Dublin, became its great prose-poet, in the stories of *Dubliners*, in the novel, *The Portrait of the Artist as a Young Man*, and in the immense epics,

Ulysses and *Finnegans Wake*. In literature, Dublin *is* James Joyce, even as London *is* Shakespeare and Charles Dickens. Our imagination of Dublin will forever be Joycean, an irony-of-ironies since Joyce rejected Dublin even as he recreated it forever.

Unlike most of his imaginative peers—Swift, Yeats, Beckett—Joyce was born a Celtic Roman Catholic, and so was not as an inheritor of the Protestant, Anglo-Saxon Ascendancy. In a sense, the contrast is between Trinity College, Dublin (Protestant) and Cardinal Newman's University College, Dublin. Joyce, educated by the Jesuits, forsook the faith, but retained the peculiar flavor of the intellectual discipline.

I myself have not been in Dublin since several extensive visits there during 1954–1955, and so I remember an eighteenth-century city essentially at one with the Dublin of Bloomsday, June 16, 1904. Friends tell me that many of the Georgian squares of Dublin no longer exist, and have become nests of skyscrapers. It will be another Oscar Wildean triumph of art over life that Dublin, old Dublin, will survive primarily as Joyce's superb invention, literature's finest fusion of naturalism and symbolism.

CHAPTER ONE

The Burden
of History

Through an intolerable heap of historical ironies, Dublin, the capital of Ireland, came to produce some of the greatest literature in the English language. Its history is labyrinthine: Dublin has seen immigrations, invasions, and emigrations; it has suffered shifts in politics, in religion; it has had times of extraordinary wealth and times of poverty; it has viewed itself with self-deprecation and chauvinism; it has been a center for nationalism and internationalism. Perhaps it has endured as much as any old town, but few cities have maintained the degree of creative intellect—and imparted such a sense of place—to project that storied history into its literature.

There is something extraordinary in this. All cities, to a certain degree, become cultural centers, drawing talented and creative individuals from the surrounding countryside. But until relatively recent times, Dublin has had little affinity to the rest of the Irish population. It never spoke Irish; its population was of English colonists and their Anglo-Irish children, who too often cared little for (or sought to be rid of) the culture of the country's Gaelic-speaking, Catholic population. Considering this, it is not so surprising that Dublin's literature has always been in English. Even the fact that Dublin's is a markedly different literary tradition from that of the rest of English literature can be explained in post-colonial terms. More intriguing is the fact that Dublin has offered up some of the *greatest* authors in the English language. By what magic had this city, a small, provincial capital for much of its history, come to engender the satires of Swift, the speeches of Burke, the plays of Sheridan and Synge and O'Casey, the lyrics of Moore, the essays of Davis, the narratives of Carleton and Stephens and O'Brien and Joyce, and the poetry of Mangan and Yeats? Something in the water, perhaps?

Around the turn of the twentieth century, William Butler Yeats became the center of a literary movement in Dublin that looked to the ancient Irish past and the folklore of the Irish peasantry for inspiration. Offshoots of this movement, despite an earlier infatuation with bucolic Ireland, found Irish character in urban Dublin. The Irish literary revival became one of the most productive periods in the history of literature, and in the course of the movement the rest of the world discovered what the Irish peasants had long known: that the people of Ireland are natural storytellers. Through the twists and turns of Dublin's story, somewhere between the Irish capacity for wit, humor, and narrative, and Dublin's struggle to identify what sort of culture it was, a unique and impressive literary tradition emerged.

Beginning with Jonathan Swift, who was the first of the great men of letters to take up the plight of the Irish, the following pages trace Dublin's literary past, and along the way offer the reader a street-level guide to the places where it happened. But while Swift himself was seminal to the culture that grew out of the city, it was Dublin that made Swift, not the other way around. And it was the warring confluence of kings and cultures that made Dublin.

ANCIENT DUBLIN

Before Dublin looked anything like a city, the place was known to the Gaelic-speaking Celts as *Baile Atha Cliath*, meaning 'town of the ford of hurdles,' referring to an ancient bridge over the river Liffey on the road between Tara and Wicklow. The Celts had arrived in Ireland in several waves of immigration, beginning around 325 B.C.E., and though a variety of cultures and tongues came over in these migrations, the Gaels soon won out.

In this Iron Age society, one's status had everything to do with one's ancestry, and with any number of petty kingdoms dividing Ireland, the need to keep track of history and genealogy was paramount. Since the language had no alphabet (Julius Caesar in fact records that writing was considered taboo) and the strange and cumbersome Ogham script did not develop until about the fourth century C.E.—even then consigned to lapidary inscriptions—an aristocratic class called the *filid* arose. It was their job to memorize old tales and histories, and, as official poets, to compose new histories about contemporary rulers. In the oldest times, the *Fili* was a man of extraordinary powers, both political and supernatural, but as the ages passed, his duties became specialized: the *filid* concerning themselves with history and poetry; the *druids* taking up the offices of magic and learning; and the *brehons* responsible for the memorization and dispensation of law. But even after the druids took over the dispensation of magic, the *filid* were dreaded for their power: the poet's curse or *aer* could ruin a man's reputation forever, and was even known to cause death.

There were seven degrees within the *filid* class: the bard, at the lowliest rung, required only seven years of instruction and memorization, whereas the highest rank, the *ollamh*, endured twelve years of study, during which he memorized hundreds of sagas and hundreds of poetic elements. According to the *Book of Ballymote*, the *ollamh* then earned the right to wear a cloak of crimson feathers, carry the wand of office, and sit as the archpoet, second only to the king.

Saint Patrick brought Christianity to Ireland sometime after 450 C.E., and with Christianity came writing. The *druid* class was eventually outlawed, only increasing the influence of the *filid* as keepers of learning. Bardic colleges were established alongside monasteries, where poets learned the strictures of meter and history, but eventually the monastic schools took the place of the bardic colleges.

Evidencing a close relationship between Christian monk and Irish poet, the old texts that come down to us consist of what the monasteries managed to transcribe and preserve. The monks compiled huge parchment and vellum books of miscellaneous material, including the great epics, genealogies, folktales, poetry, and histories, indiscriminate to the age of the source, so that one is likely to find fourteenth century biographies alongside first century sagas. The earliest surviving manuscripts are in the language of the seventh or eighth century, and it is worth noting that, contrariwise to the Christianization of the peoples on the continent, the Irish language was not Latinized, and in fact became nearly dominant within the Irish Church itself.

SAGAS AND CYCLES

The old epics took the form of sagas, divided by the *filid* into primary and secondary classes, and of the primary class the *ollamh* was required to memorize 250 separate narratives. These primary stories were further divided by their subject matter into classifications strange to modern eyes: Destruction of Fortified Places, Cattle Raids, Wooings, Battles, Stories of Caves, Navigations, Tragical Deaths, Feasts, Sieges, Adventures of Travel, Elopements, Slaughters, Water-eruptions, Expeditions, Progresses, and Visions.

Sometime during the medieval period these stories were aggregated into cycles of related eras and heroes. The mythological cycle is the earliest of these, describing the first inhabitants of Ireland as gods, good ones—the *Tuatha De Dannan*, and those of evil, the *Fomorians*, who fought amongst themselves until the Milesians (Gaels) arrived and defeated what was left of them. The second and most famous is the Ulster Cycle or Red Branch Cycle, as it is sometime called, which describes the early history of the Milesians, especially the events that surround the semi-historical King Conor, around the first century B.C.E. The Fenian or Ossianic Cycle takes place the latest, around the third century C.E., and centers on Finn MacCumhaill (MacCool) and his ancient militia, the Fianna Éirann. Stories from the Ulster and Fenian cycles are extant in the twelfth century texts, the *Book of Dun the Cow* and the *Book of Leinster*.

One of perhaps one hundred stories in the Ulster Cycle, and the most popular, is the *Táin Bó Cuáilnge* ('The Cattle-Raid of Cooley'), most recently translated by the Dublin poet Thomas Kinsella. Like much of the Cycle, the story concerns the Ulster hero Cuchulainn, who almost single-handedly routs his aggressors, the Connacht army of Queen Medb. Jealous of her husband's wealth, which includes a priceless white-horned bull, Queen Medb sends her forces to Ulster to capture the even more valuable brown bull. While the Ulster forces are stupefied under a spell, the young Cuchulainn alone defends his country, but after he faces and slays his old friend and foster brother Ferdiad in three days of battle, he cannot defend Ulster by himself. In spite of his valor, Medb's army escapes with the brown bull, which gores the white-horned bull back in Connacht, and escapes to Ulster. There, in a frenzy, the brown bull's heart explodes, and peace is made between the two kingdoms.

The Ulster Cycle also tells of the love story of Deirdre, which became a favorite of the authors of the Irish revival. Related within *The Fate of the Sons of Usnech*, the druid Cathbad prophesied at Deirdre's birth that she would become a woman of unparalleled beauty, and that many champions would fight and die for her sake. On hearing this, King Conor decided to keep the girl secluded in a mountain hut until he could take her as his wife, but as she grew older and more beautiful, she longed for the love of a man. Deirdre happened one day on Noísi, one of the sons of Usnech, with whom she fell in love, and he likewise with her. To escape the clutches of King Conor, the lovers, along with two of Noísi's brothers, ran off to Scotland, though Conor soon lured them back to Ulster. At night, while they slept in the Red Branch Palace, King Conor had it set ablaze, and in the ensuing battle Noísi and his brothers were beheaded. Deirdre took her own life, bashing her head against a rock. King Conor's behavior caused uproar throughout Ulster, and with Fergus, another hero of the kingdom, defecting to Connacht, Queen Medb found the time ripe for avenging herself of Cuchulainn. Again she sent her army into Ulster, and in one of the battles Cuchulainn was felled with a spear. He lashed himself to a rock in order to die standing up.

VIKING INVASION

Soon after Christianity vanquished the last pagans in Ireland, near the end of the eighth century, the Vikings arrived in force. In search of gold and anything else they could get their hands on, by 800 they had ransacked settlements, usually monasteries, on the islands and coastlines of the east, north, and west of Ireland. Content, at first, to rob, rape, and leave, in the first decades of the 800s Nordic fleets made their way up the rivers and into the mainland. In 836 a fleet of sixty ships sailed up the Liffey and into Meath, plundering everything from farms to churches. They sent ships into the great inland loughs, building bases from which they could attack surrounding monasteries. Fortunately, a few monks managed to escape with their precious manuscripts to mainland Europe. It is these and the compilations of the unscathed inland monasteries that have survived as ancient Irish literature, for the Vikings had no use for even the most beautiful illuminated texts.

A band of Vikings stayed in Ireland during the winter of 841–842 at a settlement along the Liffey they called Dubhlinn, which is, oddly enough, Irish for "Dark Pool," an appropriate description for that part of the river. Their settlement here was expansive, and Dublin became the base for attacks on the broader Irish countryside. In about a hundred years, the Dublin Vikings lessened their interests in raiding and started trading, a turn that made it one of the richest cities in Europe, and the envy of kings looking to expand their wealth.

It is a mistake to think that the Vikings were the only ones causing a stir in early medieval Ireland. Through the two hundred years of Viking raids, the petty kings fought with each other more than they fought the raiders, and as the Norse (who called themselves Ostmen) settled in, the Irish kings continued to wage campaigns for more and more territory.

THE EARLY KINGS

Brian Boru was the first to make himself king of all Ireland. The son of the king of Dál Cais, in north Munster, Brian acceded his throne in 976, and took the whole of Limerick and Munster within three years. While making headway into Connacht, he struck a deal with Mael Sechnaill II, the king of southern Uí Neíll, to split Ireland between the two of them, which gave Dublin and Leinster to Brian. A revolt against his rule in 999 had him at war with Sitric Silkenbeard, the king of Dublin, through that winter. Brian Boru's forces reduced Dublin to rubble, but from this victory on he had the support of the greatest city in Ireland. With Dublin behind him, he went on to make himself king of Ireland by 1011.

Governance, however, was tricky business. In the spring of 1014, a joint force of Ostmen and Leinstermen met Brian's armies at Clontarf, just outside Dublin, and though he won the battle, he fell before the fighting had ended. Brian Boru's victory at Clontarf is sometimes romanticized as a sort of Irish independence from the Viking threat, but in fact the Ostmen, by this time, were in no position to conquer the country, and the balkanization of Ireland after Brian's death, moreover, makes ridiculous any notion of Ireland as a nation.

This same balkanization was directly responsible for the introduction of Anglo-Norman rule in Ireland. After 1156, Mac Lochlainn, the king of Uí Neíll, struck an alliance with the king of Dublin and Leinster, Dermot MacMurrough, in an effort to stave off O'Conor, the king of Connacht, who was fast approaching the title of High King of Ireland. When Mac Lochlainn fell to O'Conor in 1166, Dubliners were quick to get rid of MacMurrough, whom they had never really liked anyway. (There is a story that the people of Dublin killed Dermot Mac-Murrough's father, and buried him with a dead dog underneath the town hall.) With the help of yet another king, Tighearnán O'Rourke of Bréifne, who only had one eye and whose wife MacMurrough had (quite literally) stolen, Dubliners sent Mac-Murrough packing. Dethroned and desperate, Dermot Mac-Murrough sought aid from the King of England, Henry II, who explained that while he himself could not become involved, MacMurrough would be allowed to raise an army among Henry's subjects in Wales. Dermot's new Cambro-Norman allies agreed to fight in exchange for territory, with the Earl of Pembroke, better known as Strongbow, getting a deal that included Dermot's daughter and all of Leinster after MacMur-rough's death. The Irish were no match for the invaders, who retook Dublin, Leinster, Meath, and Bréifne in just two years.

With such success, Henry became nervous that he might be facing a kingdom to rival his own, and landed in Ireland with an army in 1171. The soldiers never saw any action. Strongbow went to Henry on his knees begging for forgiveness; and the kings of Ulaid, Bréifne, Limerick, Airgialla, and Cork offered tribute. But Henry II was not interested in taking over the whole of Ireland just then—it might have been a debacle in the context of his relations with the Roman Catholic Church. Instead, he reaffirmed Strongbow in Leinster (MacMurrough had died in May 1171) and took Dublin for the Crown, leaving a certain Hugh de Lacy in charge of the city and most of Meath. He gar-risoned soldiers in Limerick and Cork, and left the country.

ENGLISH COLONIZATION AND RULE

Before the end of the century, most of Henry's original trustees in Ireland were dead, and in the course of fighting off rebellions he had won even more land, including much of Ulster. Between the kingships of Henry II and his son John, the English hold-ings were secured and granted feudally to English lords, who chose to colonize the land rather than merely tax it. In this, the lords brought with them not only soldiers, but entire settle-ments full of people, including farmers, free tenants, and arti-sans. They built new towns, and occupied the most arable lands. Irish lords were relegated to the mountains and the forests. Efforts were made to fill bishoprics within royal dioceses with Anglo-Normans, rather than Irishmen, and St. Patrick's in Dublin was established in King John's reign to train clerics that

Trinity College

Now occupying about 47 acres of Dublin's city center, Trinity College came into being when a small group of Dubliners obtained a Royal Charter for a college from Queen Elizabeth after the first University of Dublin, dating from around 1320, dis-solved during the reign of Henry VIII. In 1592, the Corporation of Dublin granted to the new institution the confiscated lands of the All Hallows monastery, about a mile outside the city walls, making Trinity Ireland's oldest institute of higher learning. Admit-tance was limited to Protestants until the relaxation of the penal laws in the early nineteenth century, and in its conception the university was intended to educate a ruling Protestant class against Roman Catholic popery.

In business now for more than four centuries, Trinity College has produced some of the greatest minds in history. Alumni of literary significance include:

Jonathan Swift, William Congreve, George Berkeley, Oliver Goldsmith, Edmund Burke, Henry Grattan, John Philpot Curran, Thomas Moore, Theobald Wolfe Tone, Robert Emmet, Thomas Davis, Charles Lever, Charles Robert Maturin, Joseph Sheridan Le Fanu, Samuel Ferguson, Bram Stoker, Oscar Wilde, Douglas Hyde, J.M. Synge, Samuel Beckett, Eavan Boland, and William Trevor.

would work with the interests of the Crown in mind. None of the remaining kings of Ireland (who kept their lands only by paying tribute to England) were granted succession of their kingdoms to heirs. Through the thirteenth and into the fourteenth century, the English colonization of Ireland was largely unchecked and almost all-encompassing.

All this time, the success of the English colonies was owing to a massive European economic boom that had populations high, labor cheap, and agriculture lucrative. But at the beginning of the fourteenth century the market finally settled down. Since their Irish lands were no longer the cash cows they had been, the lords were lured back to their English holdings. Their plantations became rundown and inefficiently worked, and what little money they produced was not reintroduced into the Irish economy but spirited away to England. Without the frequent importation of an English work force, the colonists in Ireland began to speak Irish and intermarry. English barons, quite beyond any sense of unity, waged war on each other, and even provoked their rival's Irish subjects to rise up against them. In addition to all of this, bad weather made for a series of bad harvests, which were followed by famine, which was followed by the plague, from 1348–1349. The population declined drastically, augmented by a wave of English migration from Ireland, that left farms abandoned. The ramifications of this colonization and abandonment would be felt for the duration of Irish history, well into modern times.

The Crown's attempts to reverse these trends through the 1300s were unsuccessful. Edward III implored landlords to return to their properties, to defend against rogue Anglo-Irish magnates and replant their lands. His successor, Richard II, even arrived with an army in 1394 to reassert England's power against the squabbling barons. But recolonization was an expensive prospect, and many absentees chose to sell their lands to others in Ireland instead of working to make them profitable. This only decreased English interest in the country to the west, and with the deposition of Richard II in 1399, the chances that the colonies could be brought back to their former glory were slim to none.

But this was good news for the Irish nobles, who for a time enjoyed a liberty not seen since pre-Norman days. A sort of revival set in during the fifteenth century, with bards once again singing verse about the heroic ancestors of the Irish chieftains. The Irish lords grew stronger and intermarried with the families of the Anglo-Irish overlords, and the dominion of the Crown shrunk to include only Dublin and parts of the surrounding counties, known as the Pale. Indifferent or impotent English monarchs left the governance of this area to the earls of Kildare, the FitzGeralds, though the Crown maintained a nominal claim to all Ireland.

The system was rather unruly, but it worked, and save for the constant threat of invasion of the Pale and Dublin by Irish factions, there were few complaints from either side. Then in 1534, Henry VIII, who was fresh from a particularly painful divorce, took a new interest in Ireland, especially since the ninth earl of Kildare had made it patently clear that the king's recent matrimonial developments were ecclesiastically dubious in Catholic Ireland. The king was compelled to confiscate the FitzGerald lands and execute most of the family, instituting the same religious reforms in the Irish parliament that he had in Westminster.

If Henry was looking for a good way to upset whatever political stasis there had been in eastern Ireland, he found one. Irish chieftains, once defused or otherwise contained by the earl at Kildare, sent looting bands into the Pale and Dublin, beginning a period of general tumult. Peace only settled in the Pale once the English army had pushed the most aggressive Irish leaders into the hinterlands, and made deals with the more amenable chieftains, which only amounted to the increased influence of the Crown in Ireland.

This arrangement would have been fine with the English monarchs, who were supposed to be the kings of Ireland anyway, except that maintaining garrisoned boundaries against the stubbornly independent Irish chieftains was expensive. When attempts to put the financial burden on the English citizens in the Pale failed, Queen Elizabeth looked for another solution. She got one from Sir Henry Sidney, governor of Ireland as of 1565. His was a recolonization scheme, but unlike previous endeavors of this nature, that failed because they required the expensive support of the English army for security, Sidney's put the cost on private entrepreneurs, called adventurers. Any Gaelic lords who were found to occupy the lands of the crown would be dispossessed; any Gaelic lords who took up arms against the Crown had their lands confiscated. The reclaimed lands would be subdivided and granted to the adventurers, who brought their own private armies, and who would be responsible for the establishment of English civility in their territories. If possible, genealogical evidence would be used to make claims on other territories, including those of the now-Gaelicized descendents of the original Anglo-Norman lords. The insurrections this new colonization inevitably caused among native populations were only a pretext for further land-grabbing.

These frequent revolts were a bad taste in the mouth of the Queen, and she put a stop to aggressive colonization in the 1570s, but by then a fair number of zealous English Protestants had made their homes in Ireland. It was the beginning of that terrible admixture of religious differences and land inequities that plagued Ireland into modernity.

When it became clear to Elizabeth that James Maurice FitzGerald's tiny Catholic crusade against her had support even within the Pale, martial action against him was the only option. She sent a mighty force of 8,000 men with Arthur Lord Grey de Wilton to crush the Papal forces; Edmund Spenser tagged along as Arthur's secretary, a witness, at Smerwick, in Munster, to some of the bloodiest slaughter in all the days of Ireland. When Lord Grey's work was done Spenser stayed on in Ireland, winning a sinecure in Dublin and leasing the home of Lord Baltinglas in 1581. In the summer of 1582 he began a lease in New

Abbey outside Dublin, but soon the spoils of Lord Grey's war in Munster were carved up into plantations, and in 1586 Spenser was given some 3,000 acres near Doneraile. He did not move into his new castle at Kilcolman, however, until sometime in 1588, serving in the meantime as secretary to various administrators. By 1589 he became friendly with his neighbor, Sir Walter Raleigh, with whom he shared his draft of *The Faerie Queene*. Impressed, Raleigh took the poet to meet the Queen in 1590, who gave him a pension and made him poet laureate, and on his return to Ireland Spenser settled into the life of a planter at Kilcolman. He had a second installment of *The Faerie Queene* ready for 1596, and also finished that year his *Veue of the Present State of Ireland*.

Spenser became quite familiar with misery, bloodshed, and destruction in his years in Ireland, and he drew heavily from his experiences with Irish turmoil for *The Faerie Queene*. In 1598, pandemonium came to his doorstep. Hugh O'Neill's campaign to reclaim his ancestral lands had all of Munster in rebellion that summer, and while Spenser and his family fled to Cork, his castle at Kilcolman was sacked. It was up to the poet to bring the news of the developments in Munster to the Queen, but with a heavy heart, he died three weeks after his arrival.

Twelve books were intended for *The Faerie Queene*, but at his death Spenser had finished only six and pieces of a seventh. Through his nearly twenty years in Ireland he maintained an unquestioning allegiance to the English side of things and was condescending toward the Irish themselves. Thus the heroes of his epic are Queen Elizabeth and the New English leaders in Ireland: Lord Grey is likely Artegall, Sir Walter Raleigh, Timias, and the Queen figures as Britomart, Gloriana, and Belphoebe. And since Spenser could only see the Irish as warmongering Papists, threats to English peace and Protestantism, they served as his models for wrath and lust. Specifically, the poet had the Earl of Desmond (who once held the land where Spenser ran his plantation) in mind when he wrote of Pollente, and certainly Maleger is one of the rebel O'Neills.

Hugh O'Neill's winning streak in his quest to reclaim his ancestral lands saw a tremendous English army, 20,000 men strong, dispatched to Ireland in 1601. At the Siege and Battle of Kinsale, he was simply overpowered. But O'Neill's Catholic-supported rising had been more successful than any previous threat to the authority of the Crown, and advisors convinced James I, who succeeded Elizabeth in 1603, that if he wanted Ireland to submit, the Catholics would have to be weakened. The lands of all Catholics who participated in the rebellion were confiscated, as were those of Catholics who could not show good title, in addition to any other Catholic-owned properties to which the Crown made claim. With these lands opened up for settling, the English arrived in hordes. Forward-thinking Catholics who managed to keep their holdings began to assume English dress and tongue, if only to ward off the potentially damaging suspicions held by their Protestant neighbors and officials. The complete Anglicization of Ireland was underway. Dublin, once an English-speaking outpost on foreign soil, became the administrative headquarters of Anglo-Ireland.

CHAPTER TWO

Dublin Rising

The event would be exaggerated in England, and cited for many years to justify draconian laws against the well-being of Irish Catholics. In 1641, thousands of Ulster Protestants were killed, and many thousands more were stripped of their clothing, forced to flee naked into the countryside. The typical caution of landed Irish Catholics had been forsaken, and, for once, they advocated the use of arms as a tool of negotiation with the British. But while this upper echelon of Irish society aspired to diplomacy above all to protect their interests, the rest of the Catholic populace, who had lost their lands and their dignity to the English Protestant settlers, saw in their armament a chance for vengeance.

While vicious, accounts of Irish Catholic actions were overstated in England, where the rising was made to seem widespread and downright genocidal. Roused even more so by an effective propaganda campaign, powerful English and Scots demanded action from Charles I. The king surely would have liked to quell the Irish uprising, but Charles had few friends in Parliament, and, with England at the brink of its own civil war, he could do nothing in reply.

It was the best chance in history for the Irish to rid the island of its British colonists. Colonel Owen Roe O'Neill, the nephew of Hugh O'Neill, set out to form alliances among the diverse Irish factions. He knew he needed the support of the Old English landlords to win what few centers of British power remained, but inciting this group to utter rebellion proved a tough sell. If they fought and lost, they would be left with nothing; but if they stayed on the side of the king they might yet see mercy. Lords in Leinster were ready to take Dublin—the great stronghold of the British government—but they needed the help of O'Neill. In the end, the many political factions failed to unite. When, in England, the parliamentary army succeeded against the Royalists, Ireland had Cromwell to deal with.

In spite of the scant years in which Cromwell and his cronies lorded over Ireland, they made a terrible mess. The massive social engineering schemes they began—efforts to purge the island of Roman Catholicism in the long term, and see to it that the best agricultural lands east of the Shannon were held by Protestant proprietors in the short—never were realized, troubling the country to the present day. None of it would have been possible if Cromwell hadn't been such a great general.

OLIVER CROMWELL

Cromwell began public life with a seat in the House of Commons. A devout Calvinist, he despised the power granted to priests in the Church of England, believing that each man could establish a direct relationship with God through prayer. Religion was chief among his complaints against the Crown, though he found allies among the gentry in Westminster who, like Cromwell, maintained grievances with the king regarding taxes and other threats to their financial well-being. His impeccable record of success in the English civil war was in the main due to his insistence on a well-trained, disciplined army, but Cromwell excelled in military strategy as well. After victory upon victory, he returned to the House of Commons at the end of the war in 1647; the House lauded his achievements, but thanks to tensions between the army and the Parliament, Westminster nevertheless wanted his large and powerful army dissolved. Cromwell, who believed the worst of the stories of great and terrible wrongs against Protestants in 1641, was determined to take his army to Ireland. Augmenting his cause was the widespread fear in Parliament concerning the general unrest in Ireland, a condition that had never really subsided in the years since the rising. Once King Charles I was executed and the Commonwealth declared, the need to vanquish Irish Royalists became tantamount.

The city of Dublin—England's home away from home—had been besieged by Royalist and Catholic factions, with troops numbering near 19,000. In desperation, the Governor Colonel Michael Jones led his small force of 5,000 men out of the city. He succeeded. Cromwell and his army arrived in Dublin two days later to cheers and celebration.

In just a few years, the Cromwellians won complete control of the country. Driven in part by their religious zeal, and in part by a need to avenge the actions of Catholics in the rising of 1641, they began a nation-wide program of land confiscation and conversion. Landed Catholics who could prove they had no part in the earlier rebellion were uprooted and given parcels of land west of the Shannon, in Connacht; the rest were stripped of the homesteads entirely. Catholic estates in Ulster, Leinster, and Munster became the property of Cromwell's soldiers, or the English financiers of his campaign (known as "adventurers"), or the teachers and evangelists brought in to rid Ireland of its Popish predilection.

Those evangelists might have succeeded: many priests were tried for their contributions to the rebellion, and many more fled to the Continent; but deeply held faith, an impressive language barrier, and the brevity of the Commonwealth made for an Ireland that could hardly be considered Protestant. The restoration of King Charles II in 1660—an event that at first inspired hope in the transplanted and dispossessed Catholics that they might regain their lands—only saw Cromwell's land settlement made permanent, thanks to Protestant political pressure. Thus the bulk of the land, the greatest share of the wealth, and virtually every position of power in education, ecclesiastics, and government belonged to Protestants allegiant to England, while the overwhelming majority of the populace was comprised of impoverished, Gaelic-speaking Catholics. This peculiar hegemonic structure is known as the Protestant Ascendancy, and it would dominate Ireland and Dublin for centuries to come.

In the least, a wave of moneyed, educated, Restoration Protestants brought culture to the essentially medieval town of Dublin. Dublin's first permanent stage, the Smock Alley Theatre, was founded in Dublin in 1662. The theatre was on the brink of ruin when it came to the hands of Thomas Sheridan II, who turned the Smock Alley around to the point where it rivaled the stages of London. Sheridan's father, Dr. Thomas Sheridan, was a great friend to Jonathan Swift (Swift affectionately dubbed him "Solomon," as he had nicknames for everybody, it seems), who even wrote a chunk of *Gulliver's Travels* at the Sheridan residence. Richard Brinsely Sheridan, the third generation in this literary family, would later earn a reputation in his own right as a dramatist. The Smock Alley staged plays for a hundred years before it became a warehouse, demolished later in 1811 for the construction of the Church of Saints Michael and John, on modern day Essex Street West.

JONATHAN SWIFT
Dublin had barely begun to look like other European capitals when Jonathan Swift was born, November 30, 1667. There is a plaque at the Ship Street Gate near Dublin Castle honoring his birth; the building of his traditional birthplace at no. 7 Hoey's Court is long gone, but once stood just outside the castle's western wall.

Jonathan Swift was not yet born when his father died. The elder Jonathan Swift had been a steward of the King's Inns, Dublin, after his emigration from Herefordshire, and on his death Swift, his mother, and his sister lived under the benefaction of several uncles. At six he attended the prestigious Kilkenny Grammar School, which had a reputation in those days sufficient to attract pupils from abroad. The playwright and poet William Congreve, who would become one of Swift's closest friends, attended the school around the same time, but being a few years younger the two probably did not associate. They certainly met later at Trinity College, where Swift began his studies in 1682.

At school, Swift was the archetypical class clown. He was smart but neglected his studies, given to pranks and misbehavior, obtaining his Bachelor of Arts only by *speciali gratia.* He continued on for a Master's degree at Trinity, and was just shy of his diploma when, in 1688, the whole school closed down. War had seized Ireland again.

James II was the first good thing to happen to Irish Catholics in a generation. A staunch Roman Catholic by the time he was crowned, James (rather recklessly) began reparations across the kingdom, placing Catholics in high government positions and suspending many penal laws. Many of the English in power feared James might attempt to make Roman Catholicism a state religion, and while his intentions were unclear (probably even to James), the birth of an heir and the prospect of a Catholic succession prompted English leaders to invite William of Orange, James's son-in-law, to the English throne.

Ireland was ready to fight for her king. Richard Talbot, the Duke of Tyrconnell, Lord-Lieutenant of Ireland, had had an army prepared for James's disposal (which, incidentally, caused even more hand-wringing in England). While James sought military support in France, nervous Irish Protestants threw their support to William. Notably, the towns of Derry and Enniskillen in Ulster allowed William a foothold in Ireland, while James made his way north from Kinsale in 1689. Once in Dublin, James turned Trinity College into a barracks for his soldiers, causing the temporary expulsion of all the students and faculty, including Jonathan Swift and William Congreve.

King James met the forces of William at the River Boyne in 1690. The historic Battle of the Boyne did not have to be the turning point of the war: James's forces were put on the defensive by William's advance, but he suffered few casualties and might have regrouped to fight again. Instead the King fled south all the way to France, abandoning his men and the Irish Catholic forces fighting for him. In this, the Irish Catholics were doomed in their fight. On the losing side again, they took the role of the bad guys for the next hundred years or so.

Swift and Congreve both found work in England after they were forced to leave Trinity College. Swift, now in his early twenties, began working as a secretary for Sir William Temple, an aged and important diplomat who, in his retirement, had turned to writing. Swift's task as his secretary was to help Temple prepare his memoirs, and he surely helped with Temple's other literary excursions, which included papers of literary and cultural import. Temple's *Of Ancient and Modern Learning* (1690) not only sparked the "ancients versus moderns" debate that raged at the time, but was also taken as exemplary English prose. Swift learned much from his employer's writing, taking up Temple's style and preoccupying himself with some of the same content— *The Battle of the Books*, which would be penned in the near future, is Swift's two cents on the status of contemporary learning, a compliment and defense of Temple's position.

Meanwhile, Swift met and became a tutor to Esther Johnson, a young girl also living with Temple in Surrey. She would become his "Stella," the addressee of his journals and the great love of his life, consummated or not. Stella and her companion, Rebecca Dingley, would follow Swift to Dublin in 1702. To these two ladies Swift confided his *Journal to Stella*, which contains as many details of Dr. Swift's intimacies with historical persons as it does "little language," an eyebrow-raising baby talk.

So here comes ppt aden with her little watry postscript; o Rold, dlunken Srut drink pdfr's health ten times in a molning; you are a whetter, fais I sup Mds 15 times evly molning in milk porridge. lele's fol oo now, lele's fol ee Rettle, & evly kind of Sing. (Swift, *Gulliver's Travels and Other Writings* 499)

Rumors circulated in Swift's own time as they do today as to the status of their relationship, but there never has been any real evidence of a "secret marriage."

In 1694, dissatisfied with his position and its prospects, Swift resolved to pursue a clerical career. He had begun to write, publishing first *Ode to the Athenian Society* in 1692, but it was the Church that called his attention for the time being. He was ordained a deacon in the Church of Ireland and appointed the prebend of a small church near Belfast, a depressing, run-down place. An English bishopric would do the trick: in such a post Swift could associate with the cognoscenti *and* satisfy his spiritual self. In 1696 he returned to Temple.

In 1696, Swift started writing *A Tale of a Tub*, his first great satire. The book is a flogging on two (primary) fronts: religious corruption and contemporary writers. In the story, three brothers, Peter (meant to symbolize Roman Catholics), Martin (a Protestant of the Church of England variety), and Jack (a Calvinist Dissenter) are faced with the reading of their father's (God's) will (the Bible). Each misinterprets the document in his own way, and is thus a bold exegesis of the misappropriations of religion by the major organized branches of Christianity. But all along the narrative is plagued by interruptions from the self-serving author, who, like so many writers of the day, places ridiculous, irrelevant digressions everywhere he can. Aptly named "Hack," the narrator's opinions are at the expense of the story itself, and it is clear in *A Tale of a Tub* that Hack's purpose is not to divulge the story of the three brothers, but to convey his own views, ones that could not find a forum on their own content. Hack's senselessness materializes in such pieces as "A Digression Concerning the Original, the Use, and Improvement of Maddness in a Commonwealth," and "A Digression in Praise of Digressions."

When Sir William Temple died in 1699, Swift returned to Dublin, now Chaplain to the Earl of Berkeley. In 1700 he achieved the prebend of St. Patrick's Cathedral, Dublin, a position of some importance within the Church. But if Swift's clerical career seemed racing toward the bishopric he so desired, the combined publication in 1704 of *A Tale of a Tub*, *The Battle of the Books*, and *A Discourse on the Mechanical Operation of the Spirit* was a tremendous speed bump. The volume that catapulted Swift to international literary fame was so offensive to its more pious readers, including Queen Anne, that she would never suffer him beyond the rank of Dean. It amounted to what Swift himself would term an exile of sorts. Dublin was just too far from London, the literary and intellectual center, and though the ruling Ascendancy was beginning to bring a touch of cosmopolitanism to the Pale, there were no opportunities to hobnob with the leading wits of the day. Swift remembered in one of his last works, *Verses on the Death of Dr. Swift, D.S.P.D.*:

> "In exile with a steady heart,
> He spent his life's declining part;
> Where folly, pride, and faction sway,
> Remote from St. John, Pope and Gay.

> "His friendship there to few confin'd,
> Were always of the middling kind:
> No fools of rank a mungril breed,
> Who fain would pass for Lords indeed;
> (*Gulliver's* 521)

CONGREVE AND STEELE

By contrast, William Congreve made his way to London, and was exploiting that city's possibilities by the turn of the century. He had early success with his first play, *The Old Batchelour*, and with his poem commemorating the death of Queen Mary, *Mourning Muse of Alexis*. His reputation earned Congreve the support of Charles Montagu, Earl of Halifax, the sort of real patron Swift lamented not having in the second stanza above. Montagu was able to name Congreve the Commissioner of Hackney Coaches which, whether a sinecure or not, paid £100 per year. Congreve led a life of poetry and preferments, maintaining odd government sinecures (like Commissioner to Hawkers and Peddlers and Secretary to the Island of Jamaica, among others) through Tory and Whig governments, thanks to powerful friends. After a few flops he swore off the stage, but

St. Patrick's Cathedral

Dublin already had a cathedral—the Christ Church Cathedral—when the Archbishop of Dublin, John Comyn, founded St. Patrick's beyond the city walls in 1192, outside the jurisdiction of municipal officials. The ancient church it replaced dated to the late fifth century, its foundation nearly contemporaneous with the quasi-legendary figure of Saint Patrick, and was indeed said to mark the site of a well where the patron saint of Ireland baptized Irish converts. There are lots of stories concerning Saint Patrick's ministry in Ireland, though here the deep-rooted oral tradition was bastioned in 1901 when workers clearing ground for the nearby park discovered a stone marking Saint Patrick's well.

The tale of Saint Patrick using the three-leaved shamrock to explain the concept of the trinity to the pagan Irish is often cited as evidence of his evangelical prowess, and his success in the conversion of Ireland had everything to do with his ability to show the relatedness of his new Christianity to the pagan world. The ancient Irish worshipped wells for their healing power, and after Saint Patrick and other early missionaries sanctified these places, it was easy to relate waters of healing with waters of baptismal purification.

continued to produce, appearing here and there in the periodicals of the day, like Sir Richard Steele's *Tatler*.

Steele himself was a Dubliner, born in Bull Alley north of St. Patrick's Cathedral. Like Swift, Steele was very young when his father died. Under the care of an uncle, he left for school in England at the age of thirteen, and never came back.

In London he started the *Tatler* in 1709, his first successful magazine. He went on to found, edit, and write for a host of other periodicals in the first twenty years of the eighteenth century, providing a forum for his friends, Jonathan Swift among them. From Swift Steele borrowed Sir Isaac Bickerstaff, one of a few ridiculous characters he used in his essays to prod the follies of humanity. The wit in Steele is Irish, and like Oscar Wilde in the next century, Steele took it with him when he left Dublin.

SWIFT: DEAN OF ST. PATRICK'S

It is probably true that Swift might never have been awarded the Deanery of St. Patrick's had he not been a valuable propagandist on the side of the Tories in the beginning of the eighteenth century, but it was a dubious reward at the time, since the post in Ireland eliminated any chance he would attain a post in England. Swift, by now well-respected in the literary circles of England, was ostracized from his friends Addison, Steele, and Congreve. Yet whether he liked it or not, Dublin had become his home. As early as 1710, while abroad in London, Swift wrote to his great friends Esther Johnson and Rebecca Dingley:

> Everybody asks me how I came to be so long in Ireland, as naturally as if here were my being; but no soul offers to make it so; and I protest I shall return to Dublin, and the Canal at Laracor, with more satisfaction than I ever did in my life. (*Gulliver's* 496)

Swift made the best of his station, and when the Whigs again took power in 1714, he turned his attentions to his flock. As it happened, he was very good at running his church. He initiated the celebration of the Eucharist every Sunday; he took great care of the choirs; he set aside funds to restore the Cathedral's monuments; and he even established a private bank to provide low-interest loans to the needy. So known was Swift for his charity that his congregation referred to him affectionately as "the Dane."

The Cathedral, on Patrick Street in the oldest section of town, is open to visitors and worshippers 9:00 A.M. to 6:00 P.M. most days, and services are held Sundays at 11:15 A.M.. An interested party might look in the north transept for a huge black leather chair that once accommodated the Dean's healthy posterior, and in the south aisle hang plaques marking the graves of Jonathan Swift and Esther Johnson. A tile in the floor marks the exact spot of Swift's remains, and his bust is mounted high on the left wall. A complete list of the Cathedral's hours and its full schedule of services is available online at *www.stpatrickscathedral.ie/services.htm.*

SWIFT AND NARCISSUS MARSH

Swift's lodgings while Dean were just out of spitting distance from the Cathedral, at the current site of Marsh's Library, which faces Upper Kevin Street. The oldest public library in Ireland, it was established in 1701 by Narcissus Marsh, then the Archbishop of Dublin, from his private collection. Swift knew Marsh first as a schoolboy, while Marsh was Provost of Trinity College, and with Swift's infamous indifference to his studies it is certain that he and the scholarly Marsh did not get along. Marsh wrote in his diary that he found his job as Provost, "very troublesome partly by reason of the multitude of business and impertinent visits the Provost is obliged to, and partly by reason of the ill education that the young Scholars have before they come to College whereby they are both rude and ignorant" (*www.marshlibrary.ie/marsh.html*). Marsh later stood in opposition to Swift's application for ordination, and did what he could to delay Swift's prebendship. On the other hand, Marsh was an early object of Swift's satire. He wrote that the Provost:

has the reputation of the most profound and universal learning; this is the general opinion, neither can it be easily disproved. An old rusty chest in a banker's shop, strongly locked and wonderfully heavy, is full of gold; this is the general opinion, neither can it be disproved, provided the key be lost. (Cahill 223)

The two continue their squabbles posthumously. Marsh would no doubt be pained to find among his collection of works on theology, law, medicine, science, and mathematics the personal collection of Dr. Swift, along with the table at which Swift wrote *Gulliver's Travels*, and Swift's will asks that his body lie next to the Archbishop's in St. Patrick's Cathedral. Yet the current building of Marsh's Library, built in 1781, sits squarely atop the Dean's residence and his beloved garden.

SWIFT: CHAMPION OF THE IRISH PEOPLE

It wasn't until 1720 that Swift began the sort of work that would make him a champion of the Irish in general, and of Dubliners in particular. Hyperaware, now, of the destitute conditions around him, Swift came to the conclusion that the bulk of Irish problems were due to Westminster's poor governance and England's exploitation of the country. After the passage of the malicious Declaratory Act, which reaffirmed Ireland's status of complete dependence and took all judicial power away from the Irish House of Lords, Swift had to answer. *A Proposal for the Universal Use of Irish Manufacture* was intended to rally the nation to boycott all English products. Despite inspiring a great catch-phrase ("burn everything from England but her coal") Swift failed to change Irish consumption all that much. In 1721 he began writing a series of pamphlets called the *Drapier's Letters* to circumvent the introduction of junk copper coins into the Irish monetary system. Called Wood's halfpence, the coins were a profiteering scam that started when the Duchess of Kendal won a patent from King George I (who used to be her lover) to produce Irish coinage. She sold the patent to William

Wood, owner of English tin and copper mines, who hoped to make £40,000 replacing Irish silver and gold coinage and would then kick back some of the profits to the Duchess. Swift saw real potential here for the bankruptcy of the Irish monetary system, and posing as a simple draper, he reasoned in his pamphlets for the Irish to refuse the coins. The printer of *Drapier's Letters* was arrested after a fourth installment, and the British authorities promised the impressive sum of £600 for the identity of the author. As the story goes, all Dublin knew the real identity of M.D. Drapier, but not a soul could be found to name Dr. Swift. As the Dean puts it in his *Verses on the Death of Dr. Swift*:

> Fair LIBERTY was all his cry;
> For her he stood prepared to die;
> For her he boldly stood alone;
> For her he oft exposed his own.
> Two kingdoms, just as faction led,
> Had set a price upon his head;
> But, not a traitor could be found.
> To sell him for six hundred pound.
> (*Gulliver's* 518)

Few if any used the coin, and Prime Minister Walpole was forced to buy back the patent in 1725.

GULLIVER'S TRAVELS

Swift had set aside the manuscript of *Gulliver's Travels* for a time while he took the Drapier moniker (and we may take it as evidence of a passion for his people that he delayed publication of his masterpiece to fight a copper coin), but it finally appeared in 1726. It was an instant success. Known today as a children's story, few who endeavor to read the work could imagine a child's attention outlasting the first page.

The four parts of *Gulliver's Travels* describe Lemuel Gulliver's voyages and encounters in (roughly) four different lands: first, to Lilliput, where Gulliver is a giant among a people no greater than six inches tall; second, to Brobdingnag, a land of Giants; third, to Laputa and other lands, full of irrational scientists conducting bizarre experiments; and lastly, to the Country of the Houyhnhnms, where the creatures that most resemble humans, the Yahoos, are revolting savages, and their reason-driven masters, the Houyhnhnms (pronounced who-WIN-nims, like the sound of a neigh), look like horses—the everyday slaves of human beings.

In describing the manners, customs, and troubles of the Lilliputians, Swift deftly demonstrates their shortcomings and pettiness. Gulliver, being big, acts as the moral arbiter, determining, for instance, the ridiculousness of the argument between the Big-Endians and the Little-Endians (i.e., those who prefer to crack their eggs with the big end up or vice versa), factions which symbolize Catholics and Protestants. In Brobdingnag, on the other hand, it is Gulliver who is small, and as he proudly discloses to the king the greatness of his country (England), the king asks all the right questions to show the weaknesses in British government and culture. The king and the reader conclude that Gulliver's people are at best, idiotic, and at worst, macabre.

> My little friend Gildrig [Gulliver], you have made a most admirable panegyric upon your country. You have clearly proved that ignorance, idleness, and vice are the proper ingredients for qualifying a legislator. That laws are best explained, interpreted, and applied by those whose interests and abilities lie in perverting, confounding, and eluding them. I observe among you some lines of an institution which in its original might have been tolerable; but these half erased, and the rest wholly blurred and blotted by corruptions.... I cannot but conclude the bulk of your natives to be the most pernicious race of little odious vermin that nature ever suffered to crawl upon the surface of the earth. (*Gulliver's* 134)

Most consider Part III the poorest of the book. Satirically, it targets both the bizarre experiments of the scientists of the day and the Whig followers of George I, yet instead of delineating—as the other three parts of *Gulliver's Travels* do—the best and worst of mankind, Part III is bogged down with a plethora of descriptions of goofy experiments, like turning excrement back into food (which Swift "borrowed" from Rabelais) and extracting sunbeams from cucumbers. In Swift's defense many of the studies Gulliver mentions are based on actual scientific inquiries of his time, yet the section fails to comment on human nature, except for a few misogynous quips. The fourth part, conversely, is perhaps the most sublime. Gulliver by now has come to see the foibles of his race; his encounter with the Yahoos, his repulsion by them despite their similarity to him and his kind—especially in contrast to the rational Houyhnhnms—leave him ready to quit the company of men altogether. In the end, Gulliver figures out that man is not a "reasoning creature," or *animal rationale*, as we had thought, but an *animal rationis capax*—a creature capable of reasoning.

AFTER *GULLIVER*: *A MODEST PROPOSAL*
Stella died in early 1728, and it was a terrible blow. Swift is said to have been too ill to attend her funeral at St. Patrick's Cathedral, forced to block out the windows of his nearby apartments so as not to see the memorial candles outside. After this he suffered more and more from what we now know is Ménière's disease, a disorder of the inner ear causing nausea and vertigo, which eventually drove him mad.

Yet in 1729, driven by his frustration of the Irish to unite against English oppression, Swift published his slickest, most polished satire to date, titled in full *A Modest Proposal for Preventing the Children of the Poor People in Ireland from being a Burden to their Parents or Country, and for making them beneficial to their Publick*. Without a word to waste, the pamphleteer reasons his way to one terrible solution to the abundance of impoverished children in Ireland.

> I have been assured by a very knowing American of my acquaintance in London, that a young healthy child well nursed is at a year old a most delicious, nourishing, and wholesome food, whether stewed, roasted, baked, or boiled; and I make no doubt that it will equally serve in a fricassee or a ragout. (*Gulliver's* 489)

This was the third consecutive year of bad harvests, a circumstance worsened immeasurably by the inept and absent landlords put in place after Cromwell overran the country, and by the one-sided trade policies of England, which forbade Ireland to export woolen products (its most promising commodity) to anyone anywhere, including England. In *A Modest Proposal,* Swift snarls:

> I grant this food will be somewhat dear, and therefore very proper for landlords, who, as they have already devoured most of the parents, seem to have the best title to the children. (*Gulliver's* 490)

Together with the fourth part of *Gulliver's Travels, A Modest Proposal* has had Swift labeled a misanthrope, a misnomer that began as early as Lord Orrery's *Remarks on the Life and Writings of Dr. Jonathan Swift* (1752). In a 1725 letter to Alexander Pope he clarified, "But principally I hate and detest that Animal called Man, although I heartily love John, Peter, Thomas, and so forth. This is the System upon which I have governed myself many Years (but do not tell) and so I shall go on till I have done with them" (Swift, *Dean Swift's Literary Correspondence* 29). In his life he was extraordinarily charitable, and treasured by the citizens of Dublin. It is said that Dean Swift gave a full third of his money to charity, and more remarkably he saved another third for the foundation of a hospital, an idea he had had in mind since he was a young man working for Bedlam in London. His will stipulates the purchase of a piece of land, "somewhere in or near the city of Dublin ... and in building thereon a hospital large enough for the reception of as many idiots and lunatics as the annual income of the said lands and worldly substance shall be sufficient to maintain" (Swift, *a True Copy of the Late Rev. Dr. Jonathan Swift's Will* 2).

St. Patrick's Hospital would be the first mental hospital in Ireland. Its continued operation to this date on Bow Lane and James Street is thanks to Dr. Swift's calculated instructions. He saw to it that the hospital should be exclusive to the mentally unsound, provided that an independent board of governors should see to the hospital's management, and worked closely with the architect to allow for the building's expansion.

Beyond indigents and imbeciles, Swift grew to care deeply for his countrymen. That he was Anglo-Irish—first generation to boot—and had the courage to take up the cause of the Irish in spite of his dear, English-speaking world, is his most remarkable trait. He was seemingly the first to grasp that there was a *nation* living (however poorly) outside Dublin, one that might manage its affairs without the meddling of politicians across the sea. This is not to suggest that Swift fathomed or even wanted an independent nation. His concerns were pragmatic, aimed at improving the welfare of the people on the island where he lived. Swift's villains were the men in Westminster who, say, kowtowed to the greedy English textile interests—not the English themselves. But Jonathan Swift was still a spark, the first among many literate men who would indeed try to take the cause of liberty to its logical conclusion: independence.

CHAPTER THREE

The Great Orators

The middle of the eighteenth century saw significant economic improvement for most of Ireland. Catholic-held estates in Connacht were doing well in cattle and dairy products, side-stepping trade restrictions by exporting meat to a hungry (and booming) England and butter to the Continent. The potato, a hardy and fast-growing plant, became commonplace around this time—a new and welcome form of nutrition. And there is evidence that among Catholics of a certain status the proscriptive laws codified in the Treaty of Limerick were rarely enforced or easily bypassed. This is not to say that the traditional image of the destitute Irish peasant of the eighteenth century is a fallacy. Famine as recent as 1740 had wrecked havoc on the poor population, and those lacking secure tenure were exempt from the agricultural boom that followed.

DUBLIN UNDER CONSTRUCTION

Dublin began to assume the character of contemporary cities toward the end of Swift's life. The architect George Semple, who undertook the design of Jonathan Swift's hospital, replaced the old Essex Bridge (now Grattan Bridge) with a wider one in 1755. It was not difficult thereafter for Semple to sell his plan for a wider street from the new bridge to Dublin Castle. The Wide Streets Commissioners were willed into existence by an act of the Irish parliament in 1757, and Parliament Street, as the new avenue was called, was constructed with haste. (When stubborn homeowners stood in the way of the new road's construction, the Commissioners "unroofed their houses in the middle of the night" to motivate their evacuation.) Over the century the Georgians created many more of their signature spacious boulevards, as the narrow, serpentine, medieval streets were widened and made straight. Old structures were torn down and replaced with greens and the Georgian houses that we think of as quintessential 'old town' Dublin today. The embankment of the Liffey was completed by 1757, and land recovered from the river along the quays became the sites for innumerable aristocratic homes. New bridges were built across the Liffey. Leinster House, seat of the modern Dail Eireann, parliament of the Republic of Ireland, was built in 1745. Work began in 1769 to fill in an open space at the top of Parliament Street with the Royal Exchange—today's City Hall. Trinity College saw a major facelift in this century, and many of the buildings erected during this promising time grace the campus today. The Rubrics, a set of dormitories, were finished in 1700. The Library, with its famous Long Room, was completed in 1732; since 1801 an Act of Parliament has entitled it to a free copy of every book published in England and Ireland. The Printing House, built in 1734, remains the home of the University Press, and construction on the Dining Hall was completed in 1740. Trinity College's remarkable West Front was completed in 1759, and the Provost's House in 1760. The two statues guarding the gates at Trinity College's west front, with curiously identical legs, are of Edmund Burke and Oliver Goldsmith. These treasured alumni of the University were mutual friends—though for their affinity, they made history for very different reasons.

OLIVER GOLDSMITH

Ironically, the statue of Goldsmith stands today where the aloof young man was said to have spent much of his time at Trinity College, "loitering at the College gates in the study of passing humanity," (Goldsmith xi). He was by all accounts a stupid, uncouth, ugly boy, with cash-flow problems that were accentuated after his father's death, but who would emerge as a giant of the English-speaking literary world. He was born in Roscommon sometime around 1730 (the exact date is unknown), the son of a poor cleric. As a boy Goldsmith bounced from school to school, attending a tutor at Lissoy first, but, forced to withdraw after contracting smallpox (which left him with terrible scars), he went to Elphin, then to Athlone, and finally to Edgeworthstown, before following his brother to Trinity College in 1744. It was the first time he came to Dublin, and he roomed in the Rubrics, reportedly on the top floor. Goldsmith found admittance only as a sizar, allowed to study but indentured to performing menial chores for the regular students. This situation, found also at Cambridge and Oxford in these darker days, was appalling even to the American Washington Irving as early as 1825:

> A student of this class is taught and boarded gratuitously, and has to pay but a very small sum for his room. It is expected, in return for these advantages, that he will be a diligent student, and render himself useful in a variety of ways. In Trinity College, at the time of Goldsmith's admission, several derogatory and indeed menial offices were exacted from the sizer, as if the college sought to indemnify itself for conferring benefits by inflicting indignities. He was obliged to sweep part of the courts in the morning, to carry up the dishes from the kitchen to the fellows' table, and to wait in the hall until that body had dined. His very dress marked the inferiority of the "poor student" to his happier classmates. It was a black gown of coarse stuff without sleeves, and a plain black cloth cap without a tassel. We can conceive nothing

more odious and ill-judged than these distinctions, which attached the idea of degradation to poverty, and placed the indigent youth of merit below the worthless minion of fortune. They were calculated to wound and irritate the noble mind, and to render the base mind baser. (Irving 12)

(Washington Irving was capable of any number of embellishments in his biographies—he is, for example, responsible for the story of George Washington chopping down his father's cherry tree—but this account appears to be historically accurate, as Fellow Commoners and Pensioners, the other castes of the student body, were also obliged to distinguish themselves by dress.) Goldsmith did what he could for money under these circumstances. Some friends remember him writing ballads for cash, and then stealing away to the Dublin streets to hear them sung. But while he seems to have been inclined to verse at an early age, Goldsmith was at odds to find a calling: he pursued careers in the Church, law, and education before leaving town to escape bad debts. He opted to study medicine at the University of Edinburgh.

Goldsmith left Edinburgh, too, without a degree, this time to wander the Continent on foot. When he landed in London in 1756 he somehow earned a degree in medicine, and it was only after he failed as a doctor to London's poor that he began writing seriously. He had written *The Traveler* for his brother, a longer poem, during his peregrinations in Europe. Goldsmith toiled for some years as a contributor to periodicals and pamphlets, *The Traveler* wound up in the hands of Dr. Johnson, who encouraged its publication. From here on, his writing career was successful and diverse. He was one of the first members of Samuel Johnson's inner circle, the Literary Club; he saw achievement on the stage with comedies; and he penned works on history and science. By the time of his death in 1774 he had reputation enough to earn a memorial in Westminster Abbey, one of a very few written by Samuel Johnson. As one of Trinity College's favorite sons, his statue at the gate by J.H. Foley was erected in 1864. More recently, Trinity honored him with Gold-smith Hall on the east side of the campus.

IRISH PARLIAMENT

In 1729 work began on the Parliament House at College Green, designed by the Irish architect Sir Edward Lovett Pearce. Ten years later the central part of the building was completed, making it the first building in the world of its kind—one designed for the workings of a congressional body. This was a grandiose indication of the investment Ascendancy figures were putting into their city, which, it must be remembered, was limited by its colonial status. Such limitation was the crux of the lamentations of Swift, and the overarching concern of the Ascendancy politicians from the 1750s on, many of whom were Swift's ideological inheritors. For all the grandeur of the Parliament House, the puissance of its Congress was dubious. Reinforced by the 1720 Act called 'the Sixth of George I,' the Irish parliament was ever subordinate to Westminster; a nod from London was prerequisite to any legislation. But while the real governmental authority of the Irish parliament was debated then (as it is by historians today), it was at least a vehicle for the spoken word. Thus the time was a sort of Golden Age of oration, producing men like Edmund Burke and Henry Grattan, men who spoke literature. Their recorded speeches—many of which were published soon after their delivery, evidencing their importance—contain only a glimmer of the rhetorical force they must have had when given.

But for however romantically democratic the idea of political change without political power seems today, it was a nonetheless provisional battlefield where fought the Anglo-Irish nationalists of the day. Moreover, the patriotism of this time was a peculiar form of patriotism. For the most part, their aims were Protestant and Anglophilic in a country chockablock with Catholics in a condition of servitude. With just a few rare exceptions, the Ascendancy always had both feet in England. Ultimate loyalties notwithstanding, however, the opposition to

Westminster begun by Swift and Molyneux continued with Burke, and by the time it reached Grattan and O'Connell, 'patriotism' meant fighting for *all* the denizens of Ireland.

EDMUND BURKE

Edmund Burke also wound up with Johnson, Goldsmith, and other notables in the Literary Club. He had come to London in 1753 to study law at the Temple after taking a B.A. at Trinity. Though he had breezed through his schoolwork in Dublin (unlike Goldsmith, who was likely held back a grade), he found literature now competed with the law with for his attention. Burke was born at no. 12 Arran Quay, Dublin, New Year's Day, 1729. His father, a lawyer, was a member of the Church of Ireland, while his mother was Catholic; their mixed marriage exempted the family from the Penal Laws, and Burke was raised Anglican to ensure his education. Because of his slight health, he spent a great part of his childhood in the Irish countryside with his mother's relatives. Such proximity to daily inequity must have stung the young, bright Burke, for while he lived his life ensconced in the Ascendancy, the cause of Catholic emancipation was dear to his heart. He later married a Catholic girl, Jane Nugent, no doubt adding to his awareness. As one early biographer puts it, "as she was a Roman-catholic, additional force was given by that connection to the prevailing notion of Mr. Burke's goodwill towards that communion" (Aikin 366). The rumormills of the late eighteenth century even had it that Burke was secretly baptized a Catholic, though this is unfounded.

Burke went to a Quaker school in Ballitore before returning to Dublin in 1744 to attend Trinity College. A good student, he read history, metaphysics, logic, and poetry. His father wished for Burke a career in the law, which meant London and the Temple, and his decision to write instead caused a break in their relationship for many years.

Not long in London, he found himself contributing to the city's newspapers and magazines as a supplement to his income, and won early fame in the world of letters not long after that.

His 1757 *A Philosophical Inquiry into the Origin of our Ideas of the Sublime and Beautiful* posits, in a few words, that the sublime elicits terror, and beauty elicits love. Far from a cumbersome read, the tract remains important to aesthetic theory in the present day. He also co-founded the *Annual Register* around this time, an encyclopedic summary of the year's events, the publication of which he stayed close to for over thirty years. Burke's subsequent reputation surrounded him with powerful friends, and it is their support (financial and otherwise) that allowed him his long career as a statesman. He would become one of the most vociferous members of the House of Commons, and a champion of underdogs. He used his spectacular impeachment of Warren Hastings, the governor-general of British India, to highlight the broader inequity of English Rule. He fought for the rights of American colonists, his *Speech on Conciliation with the Colonies* showing that the Crown's affront to the liberty of the colonists was an affront to liberty itself. And his brave defense of the Irish citizenry was inspired by the Enlightenment notion of the rights of all mankind. It is important to keep in mind, though, that Burke never supported (and probably could not fathom the idea of) Irish independence, despite the pedestal on which later nationalists placed him.

So what, then, made Burke a national hero? In the context of his time and station, it is fair to say he went as far as he could for Ireland: he maintained a stalwart defense of the authority of the Irish parliament; he fought for the relaxation of harmful trade restrictions; and he stood for the welfare of the vast majority of the people of Ireland.

The Penal Laws, remember, were enacted over the span of several generations, beginning in response to the uprising of 1641. While their enforcement among some classes was light, they forbade most people to pursue education, vote, practice law, teach, serve in the military, serve on a jury, hold any public office or law enforcement position, bear arms, have more than two employees (unless they were engaged in textile manufacture), and even own or transfer property. Many paid double the taxes of their Protestant neighbors. The aim—and the laws were very clear on this—was to eradicate Roman Catholicism from Ireland. Of course, even after decades on the books, the legislation had not worked. The English were creating miserable Catholics, not Anglicans.

Burke did not focus his energies on the concerns of his homeland until later in life, having spent many words defining the power of the British parliament and trying to save English face in defense of the American colonies. He failed in this, as he would fail in the fight for the Irish. Yet his speeches were of a quality not seen since the days of Cicero, perhaps, and Churchill at his best may be the nearest we have seen since. Churchill wrote that Burke was "an orator to be named with the ancients ... perhaps the greatest man that Ireland has produced" (Churchill 143–144). Woodrow Wilson characterized Burke as a man too smart for his own time to do any good:

> Everyone knows that Burke's life was spent in Parliament, and everyone knows that the eloquence he poured forth there is as deathless as our literature; and yet everyone is left to wonder in presence of the indubitable fact that he was of so little consequence in the actual direction of affairs.... If you would be a leader of men, you must lead your own generation not the next.... Burke's genius, besides, made conservative men uneasy. How *could* a man be safe who had so many ideas? (Wilson, *Leaders of Men* as posted on *http://teachingamericanhistory.org/library/index.asp? document=792*)

This is not to suggest that Edmund Burke was not appreciated in his own day. The highest praise came from the miserly Samuel Johnson, who remarked, "you could not stand five minutes with that man beneath a shed while it rained, but you must be convinced you had been standing with the greatest man you had ever yet seen" (Piozzi 209). His speeches captivated the House of Commons. Most startling is how effectively Burke could raise the debate of specific politics to something like a Platonic ideal. Takes his notes supporting free trade, for example:

> God has given the earth to the children of men, and he has undoubtedly, in giving it to them, given them what is abundantly sufficient for all their exigencies; not a scanty, but a most liberal provision for them all. The author of our nature has written it strongly in that nature, and has promulgated that same law in his written word, that man shall eat his bread by his labour; and I am persuaded, that no man, and no combination of men, for their own ideas of their particular profit, can, without impiety, undertake to say, that he *shall* not do; that they have no sort of right, either to prevent the labour, or to withhold the bread. Ireland having received no *compensation*, directly or indirectly, for any restraints on their trade, ought not, in justice or common honesty, be made subject to such restraints. (Burke, *The Beauties of the Late Right Hon* 408)

On laws forbidding the education of Catholics:

> But when we profess to restore men to the capacity for property, it is equally irrational and unjust to deny them the power of improving their minds as well as their fortunes. Indeed, I have ever thought the prohibition of the means of improving our rational nature, to be the worst species of tyranny that the insolence and perverseness of mankind ever dared to exercise. This goes to all men, in all situations, to whom education can be denied. (Burke, *A Letter from a Distinguished English Commoner* 15)

Make no mistake: these were jabs at his own coterie on behalf of people with whom he had little in common—not even the same language. By logic alone, Burke had no choice but to advocate the dissolution of the Ascendancy.

The Protestants of Ireland are not *alone* sufficiently the people to form a democracy; and they are too *numerous* to answer the ends and purposes of an *aristocracy*. Admiration, that first source of obedience, can be only the claim or the imposture of the few. I hold it absolutely impossible for two millions of plebeians, (Catholics) composing certainly, a very clear and decided majority in that class, to become so far in love with six or seven hundred thousand of their fellow-citizens (to all outward appearance plebeians like themselves, and many of them tradesmen, servants, and otherwise inferior to some of them) as to see with satisfaction, or even with patience, an exclusive power vested in them, by which *constitutionally* they become the absolute masters; and by the manners derived from their circumstances, must be capable of exercising upon them daily and hourly, an insulting and vexatious superiority. Neither are the majority of the Irish indemnified (as in some aristocracies) for this state of humiliating vassalage (often inverting the nature of things and relations) by having the lower walks of industry wholly abandoned to them. They are rivaled, to say the least of the matter, in every laborious and lucrative course of life: while every franchise, every honour, every trust, every place down to the very lowest and least confidential (besides whole professions) is reserved for the master cast. (*Beauties of the Late Right Hon* 139)

If Burke had had his way, it would have meant the end of a system of hegemony too cozy for most of his peers to give up. (Indeed, it is on this humongous issue that Burke ended his friendship with that other Ascendancy nationalist, Henry Flood, who fought like a lion for the rights of the Irish parliament but could not stomach raising Irish Catholics to his level.) For all his failures to ameliorate the quality of Irish life, however, Burke was seminal to the cause of Irish liberty. And yet those who would claim to be descendants of Burke's nationalism—the likes of Thomas Davis and others fighting for Irish independence discussed later in this text—were arguing for something much different.

RICHARD BRINSLEY SHERIDAN

One of Burke's shining moments in the House of Commons was the impeachment of Warren Hastings, whom Burke accused of mismanaging English rule in India. Aiding Burke in this cause was a fellow Dubliner, who, while capable of a jaw-dropping five-hour speech (after which the House of Lords had to break to quell their emotions), did not "waste his talents," like Burke, in Parliamentary affairs. By the time Richard Brinsley Sheridan had landed a seat in the House of Commons, he had written eight lucrative plays and was managing London's Drury Lane theatre. Sheridan's celestial success on the stage led many to consider him the best comedic playwright since Shakespeare.

Sheridan was born in north Dublin, at no. 12 Dorset Street Lower, in 1751, and baptized at St. Mary's Protestant Church at the corner of Mary and Jervis Streets. His mother Frances, née Chamberlaine, was also Dublin-born, and a novelist and play-wright of some repute. She met Richard's father Thomas in connection with the Smock Alley Theatre (Dublin's oldest stage) where he was an actor and manager after graduating from Trinity College.

There was trouble in the theatre. During a staging of Voltaire's *Mahomet the Imposter*, the actors sought to extend the play with a politicized encore—it would have been a trans-parent comment on English rule. Thomas Sheridan would not have it; he opted not to compromise aesthetics with politics. In response the actors rioted in the theatre, tearing up the cloth backdrops with their prop swords and overturning the benches. The riot lasted six hours, driving their manager from the city. He returned a few years later to resume management of the the-atre, but by then a competing stage had sprung up in Dublin—that of Barry and Woodward—prompting Thomas Sheridan to take his family to England. His youngest son Richard would never return to the city of his birth.

Richard Brinsley Sheridan had but a little education at Sam Whyte's grammar school in Dublin, which sat at no. 79 Grafton St. In England he was sent to Harrow's, where he did poorly. After a storybook escape to France, a secret marriage, and a duel, he married into some money, and it was his socialite friends that persuaded him to write plays. In this he had quick success. He was but twenty-four when *The Rivals* was staged at Covent Garden. By 1776 he was managing Drury Lane. Mostly comedies and farces, his plays were huge hits in London, but as time went on it became harder for Sheridan to create with the quality and speed his public was used to. His contributions to Whig journals surrounded him with the sort of people who could help him win a seat in the House of Commons for Stafford in 1780.

Sheridan's shift to politics was an exit strategy of sorts, and a logical move at the time. Surely his experience in stagecraft lent to Sheridan's talents as an orator—a skill so important in the Parliament of the time. His reputation in this capacity soon rivaled that of Burke. Lord Byron (who was, admittedly, Sheridan's drinking buddy) declared Sheridan's speech during the impeachment proceedings of Warren Hastings (his "Begum Speech") his crowning achievement, "the very best Oration ... ever conceived or heard in this country" (Byron 239). Tickets were sold to the event in Westminster Hall in true mimicry of the stage, and the attendees, who paid 50 guineas each for entry, are said to have balled at Sheridan's performance. But critics of his political move accused him of lacking conviction, and they were probably right. His Begum speech really was Sheridan's crowning achievement, having become insignificant in parliamentary affairs thereafter. He died in abject poverty, 1816, with more foes than friends.

HENRY GRATTAN

Henry Grattan, another Dubliner-politician, famed as an orator, could never be accused of insincerity in his work. Grattan (1746–1820) actually won an independent Irish

Parliament—the aim of so many for so long—only to have it taken away by the treachery of a fellow Trinity College alumnus.

Most biographers fix Grattan's place of birth in Belcamp, just north of the city center, though the exact date and place are unknown. Written records confirm for sure, though, that he was baptized on July 3, 1746, at St. John's Church at the upper end of Fishamble Street, where his father lived for many years. This church, also said to be the site of the burial of that legendary fishmonger of song, Molly Malone, is gone like so much of Dublin's antiquity. He went to the schools of Mr. Ball in Great Ship Street, and Mr. Young in Abbey Street before entering Trinity College. Grattan was called to the bar after his days at the university, and when he won a seat in the Irish parliament, he took to task the reform of Irish trade laws and parliamentary independence. This was in line with the concerns of Edmund Burke, certainly Grattan's ideological predecessor, but where Burke might be considered an Irish nationalist, Grattan was an Irish republican. Here lies the paradigm shift with Grattan and O'Connell, and others active just a generation after Swift's death: Catholic emancipation was not an end in itself; it was instead a means to Ireland's independence.

Thanks to his skillful oratory, augmented by a 100,000-man-strong martial threat called the Volunteers, and inspired by the success of the American Revolution, Grattan won an independent Irish parliament with his Declaration of Rights in 1782. His victory speech is a summation of Ireland's long struggle to this moment:

> I am now to address a free people: ages have passed away, and this is the first moment in which you could be distinguished by that appellation.
>
> I have spoken on the subject of your liberty so often, that I have nothing to add, and have only to admire by what heaven-directed steps you have proceeded until the whole faculty of the nation is braced up to the act of her own deliverance.

I found Ireland on her knees, I watched over her with a paternal solicitude; I have traced her progress from injuries to arms, and from arms to liberty. Spirit of Swift! spirit of Molyneux! your genius has prevailed! Ireland is now a nation! In that new character I hail her! and bowing to her august presence, I say, Esto perpetua!

She is no longer a wretched colony, returning thanks to her governor for his rapine, and to her King for his oppression; nor is she now a squabbling, fretful sectary, perplexing her little wits, and firing her furious statutes with bigotry, sophistry, disabilities and death, to transmit to posterity insignificance and war....

You, with difficulties innumerable, with dangers not a few, have done what your ancestors wished, but could not accomplish; and what your posterity may preserve, but will never equal: you have moulded the jarring elements of your country into a nation ... you had not the advantages which were common to other great countries; no monuments, no trophies, none of those outward and visible signs of greatness, such as inspire mankind and connect the ambition of the age which is coming on with the example of that going off, and form the descent and concatenation of glory: no, you have not had any great act recorded among all your misfortunes, nor have you one public tomb to assemble the crowd, and speak to the living the language of integrity and freedom.

Your historians did not supply the want of monuments; on the contrary, these narrators of your misfortunes, who should have felt for your wrongs, and have punished your oppressions with oppressions, natural scourges, the moral indignation of history, compromised with public villainy and trembled; they excited your violence, they suppressed your provocation, and wrote in the chain which entrammelled their country. I am come to break that chain, and I congratulate my country, who, without any of the advantages I speak of, going forth, as it were, with nothing but a stone and a sling, and what oppression could not take away—the favour of Heaven, accomplished her own redemption, and left you nothing to add and everything to admire. (Madden 70–71)

Grattan had every reason to rejoice in the occasion, and his heartfelt speech is bereft of exaggeration. In thanks the House of Commons blessed Grattan with the sum of £50,000 for his services, which he used to purchase an estate in the country. In his will he instructed that, in the event his children die without progeny of their own (which never happened) his estate should be placed "in trust to form a foundation for the annual support of unprovided gentlewomen, daughters of poor and meritorious citizens of Dublin."

Thus the Palladian structure that is now the Bank of Ireland was known as Grattan's parliament. Nearby at no. 3 College Green, the building with the grey façade that now houses the National Assurance Company, was once part Daly's Club, one of this parliamentarian's favorite stomping grounds. A den of high-limit gambling, Daly's had formerly been connected to the western portico of the Parliament House for the convenience of its many constituents there. Along with that other literary patriot, Thomas Davis, Grattan's statue stands in the center of College Green. The park, a one-time Viking burial ground, was home for a time to an equestrian statue of William III, but, subjected to any number of degradations from Dublin's thankless citizenry (students at nearby Trinity College have always been prime suspects), the statue was blown up in 1829. A restored monument was likewise blown to bits in 1929, never to return.

Too bad for Grattan and everybody else, the Irish Parliament was still subordinate to the Crown and the Dublin Castle executive, making it difficult to exercise the sort of power he might have imagined. Too bad, moreover, Grattan's gains prompted a conservative backlash (for a time at least) within the Irish Parliament itself, frustrating any advances in the fight for Catholic rights. And too bad all his work would soon be undone. As was entirely possible in those days, the bulk of the Irish Parliament was bought off by Robert Stewart, Lord Castlereagh, to vote its own destruction: to vote Union.

ACT OF UNION AND THE DECLINE OF DUBLIN

By the 1790s, Westminster had to do something about the

John, Robert, and Sarah

The Cork-born John Philpot Curran came to Dublin to attend Trinity College, began his career in law in 1775, and overcame difficulties with public speaking to become one of the most gifted orators of the eighteenth century. As a barrister his wit was matched only by his courage. He took to the defense of Hamilton Rowan, Theobald Wolfe Tone, Lord Edward Fitzgerald, and other leaders of the rising of 1798 in a time when courts were corrupt, bribery was commonplace, and saber-rattling was quite serious. For much of his public life Curran championed Irish liberty and Catholic emancipation, and was vehemently anti-Union in the last years of the century, though he would never support armed rebellion.

Curran's convictions led him to forbid his daughter Sarah to continue her relationship with the young rebel Robert Emmet, but the two were in love and carried on their correspondence in secret. To keep their relationship (and later engagement) hidden from her father, Sarah often wrote to Robert in code and left her letters unsigned. When Emmet was arrested in Dublin on a visit to Sarah, authorities confiscated all the anonymous love letters he was keeping in his coat, and demanded the name of his love. Emmet managed to keep Sarah's identity quiet through his trial, but in the fall of 1803 he was betrayed by his jailor. While soldiers searched the Curran house downstairs, Sarah's sister burned Robert's letters upstairs. Enraged, John Curran disowned Sarah, who fled to Cork. Emmet was hanged, drawn, and quartered the day after his famous *Speech from the Dock*.

situation in Ireland. The United Irishmen, begun in 1791 as an intellectual debate group, was taking notes from the revolutionary movement in France, ready to stage their own insurrection; the cities were abuzz with rebellion; and Britain, at war with France, had too few troops across the Irish Sea for comfort. As it happened, the rebellion, envisioned by Theobald Wolfe Tone and the United Irishmen as a joint effort by disparate factions, was doused by an early sweep of rebel strongholds, and was an utter failure. In truth the 1801 Act of Union was supposed to wrap up neatly and dispose of all Ireland's troubles. Catholic emancipation was promised. Ireland would have free trade with Britain. The Irish would have representation at Westminster, but the Irish Parliament would be dissolved.

There were riots in Dublin. Henry Grattan wound up in a duel with the Lord Chancellor; he shot the latter in the hand.

The effects of this on Dublin cannot be overstated. Having lost its status as a world capital, and having little else to sustain its economy, the city entered a period of decline not to be reversed until the twentieth century. The elite left town, most for London, and took with them their culture and their money. Much of the city's trade had been supported by its demand for luxury goods, which vanished with the rich. Those with money began building in the suburbs, accentuating the poverty of the city center. The jails filled with debtors. The Georgian houses emptied, lost their value, and became slums as Dublin's population continued to rise, resulting in the strange sight of the destitute living in rundown homes with marble entryways and grand staircases. The purpose and power of the Wide Streets Commissioners, the group responsible for civic improvement, waned slowly, but the commission was at last abolished in 1841. Plans were even drafted to fill in St. Stephen's Green with housing, but luckily this was never realized. The Parliament House, built with such hope, was sold to the Bank of Ireland for £40,000, and the British government decreed that its interior be remodeled to proscribe any future use of the building as a house of debate. This last transformation only served as a ghostly reminder of *what might have been* to the disenfranchised Dubliners of the years following. James Joyce evokes its memory in *A Portrait of the Artist as a Young Man*:

> Mr Dedalus lingered in the hall gazing about him and up at the roof and telling Stephen, who urged him to come out, that they were standing in the house of commons of the old Irish parliament.
>
> —God help us! He said piously, to think of the men of those times, Stephen, Hely Hutchinson and Flood and Henry Grattan and Charles Kendal Bushe, and the noblemen we have now, leaders of the Irish people at home and abroad. Why, by God, they wouldn't be seen dead in a tenacre field with them. No, Stephen, old chap, I'm sorry to say that they are only as I roved out one fine May morning in the merry month of sweet July. (Joyce, *A Portrait of the Artist as a Young Man* 96–97)

To add insult to injury, the promises of Catholic equity went unfulfilled. Irish Catholics were still not on even footing with the Protestants after the Act of Union, especially in positions of power. The need for real civil rights called the remarkable Daniel O'Connell into history. He wasn't born in Dublin, nor did he go to school there. Nonetheless, he was elected that city's Lord Mayor in 1824, and Sackville Street, the main thoroughfare of the metropolis, was renamed in his honor. His statue by J.H. Foley is near the bridge on that street. For much of his time in Dublin, this "Uncrowned King of Ireland" lived at no. 58 in the upscale Merrion Square.

O'Connell was from an old aristocratic family in Kerry, which was nevertheless in dire straits from the effects of the Penal Laws. A lawyer-scholar, his first public appearance came in 1800, when he delivered to a Dublin crowd an invective on the proposed Act of Union, wherein he boldly proclaimed that given the choice between Union and the Penal Laws, Catholics would choose the disparaging laws. His rise to the appellation of

"Liberator" began with his involvement in the Catholic Association in 1823. Fueled by the need for civil reform among Catholic populations, O'Connell did his work not in legislatures (the law saw to that) but in massive public forums. This was democracy by definition. At the Corn Exchange Building on Burgh Quay, Dublin, O'Connell set up shop. His massive grassroots organization, aided by Catholic clergy all over Ireland, was a sort of boot camp, providing Catholics with the tools to take leadership positions. And here Daniel O'Connell may have had more influence on Irish literature than anyone in history: he advocated the use of the English language. Speaking English would help to modernize the country, he thought, and only make the peaceful fight for independence easier. O'Connell's advice, combined with the devastating effects of the Famine of 1848 on Ireland's population, was dramatic: Gaelic had to be "remembered" by the revivalists of the nineteenth century.

His group won Catholic rights to sit in Parliament in 1829, and moved on to Westminster to repeal the Act of Union. Establishing Protestant alliances in this proved difficult, despite the tremendous support of the Irish people. O'Connell's longtime foe, Sir Robert Peel, finally had him imprisoned in 1844, and though he was soon released, the experience ruined his health. Regardless of the good works O'Connell accomplished in London, his lack of results lit fires under the more hasty Young Irelanders, a group who once again would take up arms for their cause.

CHAPTER FOUR

The Early Novelists

MARIA EDGEWORTH

To Maria Edgeworth goes the honor of writing the first novel proper to come out of Ireland. Though born in England, she spent most of her life at her family's large estate in Edgeworthstown, some seventy miles from Dublin. The family was an old one, first settling in Ireland in Elizabethan days, and for centuries had been landed in County Longford around the town that bears their name. She was the second issue and eldest daughter of Richard Lovell Edgeworth, an eclectic and influential man, Trinity College alumnus, inventor, and statesman, known for his work to bring the telegraph to Ireland and for being an outspoken advocate of Union with England. But he also dabbled in writing, criticism, and education. With his hands in all this, Richard Edgeworth needed help, and Maria became his collaborator in most everything, but especially in his writing.

Remarkably—and indicative of Maria's intellect and education—Richard sired twenty-two children in his days, and Maria was not, as one might expect, relegated to the task of overseeing a household with so many youngsters. It is appropriate, however, that her first published literary endeavor is *The Parent's Assistant*, a full six volumes of stories contrived to occupy the herd of children around the Edgeworth estate. Four years later she had finished *Castle Rackrent* (1800). An admonition on the perils of poor stewardship of Irish landlords, the novel depicts several generations of the Rackrent family, whose name Edgeworth took from the practice of charging tenants a rent as high as the value of the land itself. *Castle Rackrent* is told with enough innovation—it is, for instance, the first book of its kind to span generations—to earn a place in the development of the novel; but chroniclers of literary history never fail to mention the influence of Richard Edgeworth, who was rumored to have maintained a strict oversight of Maria's writing. Claims of any real redaction on the part of Edgeworth the father are largely unsubstantiated, stemming from a dubious early biography written by Maria's stepmother and stepsisters, but there is no doubt that Maria thought the world of her father's opinions. The best evidence of his influence is the very substance of her novels. *Castle Rackrent* and *The Absentee*, among other novels set in Ireland, read at times like anecdotal evidence supporting her father's politics.

As a prominent landowner, Richard Edgeworth concerned himself with the reform of the exploitive relationship between landlord and tenant in those days, which was still fraught with unbearable rents for tiny parcels of land, making profit for most tenant farmers impossible. Even worse for the Irish farmer was the institution of absentee landlordship, which had been going on since Cromwell's day, wherein (mostly Protestant) landowners lived in England away from the cares of their property, taking the proceeds out of Ireland's economy altogether. Edgeworth sought to repair this system locally by example: he took pains to treat his Catholic tenants fairly. On a larger level it informed his support of Union with England: Irish representation in Westminster would bring security, and security would induce rich English families to maintain at least temporary homes in Ireland, rousing new interest in the welfare of their lands and the people working them. In a pro-Union speech before the House of Commons of the Irish Parliament in 1800,

Edgeworth claimed that the Act of Union would give English landowners a renewed stake in the future of their estates in Ireland, and that "younger branches of opulent families may represent themselves in this country, to manage, and perhaps inherit their family estates" (Richard Edgeworth 7).

The vision of the young noble returning to his family's Irish estate is precisely the plot of Maria Edgeworth's *The Absentee* (1809). Lord Colambre, the hero, has been schooled at Cambridge in the ways of a fine English gentleman, but despite the wishes of his myopic mother—who is hostile toward all things Irish—he sees that skilled oversight of the family's Irish estate could be a boon to their precarious financial situation. Moreover, Colambre has a sense of connection to the place of his birth, of which he has but fleeting memories. "[H]is own country was endeared to him by early association," Edgeworth writes early in the novel, "and a sense of duty and patriotism attached him early to Ireland" (Maria Edgeworth 6). In London's streets, Lord Colambre delights in hearing the charming brogue and vivacious speech of Irish workmen. Along with a degree of independent thinking, it is enough to make him wonder, "Shall I too be an absentee?" (76). By the end of the fifth chapter, Colambre tires of the contradicting accounts of the Irish he hears in London, resolving to judge Ireland and her inhabitants for himself.

Colambre lands in Dublin, and it is here in Chapter VI that Edgeworth sets the bulk of the book's post-Union Dublin scenes. On shore, Colambre meets first the downtrodden citizens of Dublin, scraping for what few pennies they can get from the English lord. Their frenzy and need dispel away the idyllic visions he had fostered, "and if his heart swelled, it swelled no more with pleasurable sensations, for instantly he found himself surrounded and attacked by a swarm of beggars and harpies, with strange figures and stranger tones; some craving his charity, some snatching away his luggage, and at the same time bidding him 'never trouble himself,' and 'never fear'" (77). This is Edgeworth's allowance of the social conditions in post-Union

Dublin. Of course, the author was not out to portray Ireland in a negative light; when Colambre reaches his Dublin hotel, he finds all his luggage intact, and a few pennies to his makeshift porters earn him gratitude and smiles. It is important to note that in this early stage of the development of the novel, Edgeworth will always compromise verisimilitude for didacticism. In the city Colambre meets and befriends an officer, Sir James Brooke, whom Edgeworth presents as an authority on the politics of Ireland. To counter the complaints of a lady in the company who is peeved by the uncouth nouveaux riches all around town, Sir James gives this synopsis of the effects of the Act of Union:

> I happened ... to be quartered in Dublin soon after the Union took place; and I remember the great, but transient change, that appeared from the removal of both houses of parliament: most of the nobility and many of the principal families among the Irish commoners, either hurried in high hopes to London, or retired disgusted and in despair to their houses in the country. Immediately, in Dublin, commerce rose into the vacated seats of rank; wealth rose into the place of birth. New faces and new equipages appeared: people, who had never been heard of before, started into notice, pushed themselves forward, not scrupling to elbow their way even at the castle; and they were presented to my lord-lieutenant and to my lady-lieutenant; for their excellencies, for the time being, might have played their vice-regal parts to empty benches, had they not admitted such persons for the moment to fill their court. Those of former times, of hereditary pretensions and high-bred minds and manners, were scandalized at all this; and they complained with justice, that the whole *tone* of society was altered; that the decorum, elegance, polish, and charm of society was gone. And I among the rest ... felt and deplored their change.(80)

In his speeches to the Irish Parliament in favor of Union, Richard Edgeworth granted that the effects of the legislation on

Dublin would be minor, but only for a time: after a period of hardship, Dublin would emerge with more status than it could ever achieve as a provincial capital:

> I am willing to allow, that in this city undoubtedly one source of traffick will be dried up; but will not increased habits of parsimony and attention to business balance the loss?—Tradesmen copy those whom they serve. A taylor and a milliner are generally extravagant; a wholesale dealer generally provident—Dublin, as a commercial city will, in all probability, be in twenty years a richer city than it could be as the seat of vice-regal magnificence. (Richard Edgeworth 11)

Thus, Sir James Brooke explains how much better Dublin became. His description is an Edgeworthian prediction of a new, cosmopolitan Dublin:

> But, now it's all over, we may acknowledge, that, perhaps, even those things which we felt most disagreeable at the time, were productive of eventual benefit.
>
> Formerly, a few families had set the fashion. From time immemorial everything had, in Dublin, been submitted to their hereditary authority; and conversation, though it had been rendered polite by their example, was, at the same time, limited within narrow bounds. Young people, educated upon a more enlarged plan, in time grew up; and, no authority or fashion forbidding it, necessarily rose to their just place, and enjoyed their due influence in society. (Maria Edgeworth 80)

The uncouth, unschooled new money—the thorn in the side of the weakening landed gentry of the nineteenth century—would self destruct:

> The want of manners, joined to the want of knowledge, in the *nouveaux riches*, created universal disgust: they were compelled, some by ridicule, some by bankruptcies, to fall back

into their former places, from which they could never more emerge. (80)

Those who left Dublin with its erstwhile parliament would become homesick:

> In the mean time, some of the Irish nobility and gentry, who had been living at an unusual expense in London—an expense beyond their incomes—were glad to return home to refit; and they brought with them a new stock of ideas, and some taste for science and literature, which, within these latter years, have become fashionable, indeed indispensable, in London. That part of the Irish aristocracy, who, immediately upon the first incursions of the vulgarians, had fled in despair to their fastnesses in the country, hearing of the improvements which had gradually taken place in society, and assured of the final expulsion of the barbarians, ventured from their retreats, and returned to their posts in town. (81)

It all would lead to the creation in Dublin of a real democratic society, unlike anything one might find in London:

> "So that now," concluded Sir James, "you find a society in Dublin composed of a most agreeable and salutary mixture of birth and education, gentility and knowledge, manner and matter; and you see pervading the whole new life and energy, new talent, new ambition, a desire and a determination to improve and be improved—a perception, that higher distinction can now be obtained in almost all company, by genius and merit, than by airs and address ... So much for the higher order. Now, among the class of tradesmen and shopkeepers, you may amuse yourself, my lord, with marking the difference between them and persons of the same rank in London." (81)

Things did not work out as the Edgeworths planned.

After her father's death, Maria took over the affairs of the Edgeworth estate, and found it difficult to continue writing. While the absence of her father's critical eye was partly to blame, the deteriorating state of affairs in Ireland made it impossible for her to stomach portraying her country with any degree of mimesis. It was not that Maria Edgeworth was so separated by money and resentment in the decades after Union that real portraits of the Irish were beyond her powers; the fact is that conditions had deteriorated such that writing real life was too gruesome for her to endure. She and her father had labored in their *Essay on Irish Bulls* to rid English fiction of its Irish stereotypes, or stage-Irishmen, as these characters were called. At issue was the depiction of the Irish people as they really were—not merely whisky-soaked, banshee-fearing props ushered in for comic relief. Castle Rackrent was heavily footnoted in the interest of instructing of English readers. But by the third decade into the nineteenth century, "real Ireland" was too lurid for her style of fiction. "It is impossible," she wrote to her brother in 1834, "to draw Ireland as she is now in a book of fiction—realities are too strong, party passions are too violent to bear to see, or care to look at, their faces in the looking glass" (Hare 202). When the Great Famine of 1845 set in—a catastrophe which surely, above all, countered any of the gains the Edgeworths hoped would follow Union with England—Maria did everything she could for the residents of Edgeworthstown. Her zealous philanthropy was emaciating. She died before the famine had run its course, in 1849.

SAMUEL LOVER AND CHARLES LEVER

Indeed, the strong and terrible realities of nineteenth century Ireland can be blamed for the popularity of two Dublin authors, Samuel Lover and Charles Lever, who chose to abandon Irish verisimilitude in their novels, embracing instead the portrait of the stage-Irishman in the pursuit of lighthearted distraction. The American scholar Maurice Francis Egan had it right when he wrote that Lover exhibits "a habit of patronizing the Irish." "The chief defect of [Lover's] novels ... is that they were written with an eye on what the English reader would expect Irish characters to do" (Egan 329). A passage from Lover's *Handy Andy* (1842), though hilarious, demonstrates precisely the conventions of the stage-Irish:

> "Do you feel your knee better now, sir?" asked one of the party, of Murphy.
>
> "Considerably, thank you; whisky punch, sir, is about the best cure for bruises or dislocations a man can take."
>
> "I doubt that, sir," said a little matter-of-fact man, who had now interposed his reasonable doubts for the twentieth time during Murphy's various extravagant declarations, and the interruption only made Murphy romance the more.
>
> "*You* speak of your fiery *Dublin* stuff, sir; but our country whisky is as mild as milk, and far more wholesome; then, sir, our fine air alone would cure half the complaints without a grain of physic."
>
> "I doubt that, sir!" said the little man.
>
> "I assure you, sir, a friend of my own from town came down here last spring on crutches, and from merely following a light whisky diet and sleeping with his window open, he was able to dance at the race ball in a fortnight; as for this knee of mine, it's a trifle, though it was a bad upset too."
>
> "How did it happen, sir? Was it your horse—or your harness—or your gig—or—"
>
> "None o' them, sir; it was a *Banshee.*"
>
> "A Banshee!" said the little man; "what's that?"
>
> "A peculiar sort of supernatural creature that is common here, sir. She was squatted down on one side of the road, and my mare shied at her, and being a spirited little thing, she attempted to jump the ditch and missed it in the dark."
>
> "Jump a ditch, with a gig after her, sir?" said the little man.

"Oh, common enough to do that here, sir; she'd have done it easy in the daylight, but she could not measure her distance in the dark, and bang she went into the ditch: but it's a trifle, after all. I am generally run over four or five times a year."

"And you alive to tell it!" said the little man, incredulously.

"It's hard to kill us here, sir, we are used to accidents." (Lover 221)

Lover had more sentiment for the Irish than Lever, but both got famous exploiting the Irish peasant and were never worried about realism. Edgeworth and (later) Carleton understood the harm in this: the novels of Lover and Lever only reinforced the prejudices of an English readership, when what was really needed was attention to a quickly deteriorating society.

Charles Lever was born in the North Strand, at what is now 35 Amiens Street, in 1806. Some biographers list his father a carpenter by trade, but James Lever was really a builder, and in those days there was a thin line between builder and architect. He worked closely with Francis Johnston on the General Post Office and on the conversion of the Parliament House into the Bank of Ireland. Lever's mother was from a family that benefited from the Cromwellian land grab, and young Charles grew up on the side of the Tory and the Protestant, with little regard for the other parties. He was a witty and mischievous boy, a good storyteller and a bit of a ham, whose friends recall a particularly good impression of Daniel O'Connell. He had a reputation for idleness in the Dublin schools, as he hated to read and study, but he won over the hearts of many schoolmasters with his "silver tongue." At Trinity College around 1830, disappointed with the lack of society in the city, he formed the Burschenschaft, a goofy club with pseudo-intellectual pursuits, silly German costumes, and bizarre titles like "Hereditary Bearer of the Wooden Spoon." Lever was elected their Grand Lama, though, under his leadership the club spent more time drinking than they did discussing topics of intellectual merit. Still, it was in the presence of this society that many of the comical ballads and lyrics of Lever's later works had their first airing. He took his degree in medicine in 1831 and set up a practice at his father's house on Talbot Street, but he saw few maladies and little income. When the cholera epidemic broke in the West in 1832, Lever was summoned to help like so many young doctors. To his credit, he picked up and went to Clare, bravely fighting a disease that no one knew how to treat. Accounts of his success—both in saving some of the afflicted and in not contracting the disease himself—cite his humor and high spirits as key to his survival. The folks he met in Clare, and moreover, their stories, became the stuff of his novels. Perhaps given the effects Lever's good humor exacted in his personal life, he may be exonerated for treating Irish life with impossible gaiety.

Lever began contributing to Dublin magazines in the late 1830s. His *Harry Lorrequer*, the first of thirty novels, was serialized in the *Dublin University Magazine* in 1839. He became editor of that publication in 1842, the same year he came to live in the famous Templeogue House in the South Dublin suburbs. Supposedly haunted, the house is said to have been the refuge of King James on the night he lost the Battle of the Boyne, and a sanctuary for the Knights Templar before that. Lever stayed here only a few years, leaving Dublin and the magazine for Italy in 1845, only returning to Ireland on occasion.

Lover, the son of a stockbroker, was born at no. 60 Grafton Street, and gave up plans to pursue the profession of his father when a career as a painter of portraits and miniatures unfolded before him. On his own, he lived for a time at 9 D'Olier Street, where he compiled and illustrated a volume of Irish folktales entitled *Legends and Stories of Ireland* (1831). None of these tales could be construed as derogatory, but the characters are mostly comical. He possessed equal talent as a singer and writer of songs and ballads, and was probably more famous for his songs (he wrote more than 300) than for his novels. In London after 1835, he turned his ballad *Rory O'More* into a novel, and

The Orange Order

Better known as the Orangemen, the Orange Order was first organized in northern Ireland in 1795, named in honor of William of Orange and his decisive victory at the Battle of the Boyne one hundred years earlier. The association emerged as a Protestant response to the juggernaut of pro-Catholic political entities such as the United Irishmen and other once-secret societies called Defenderists. Such groups had campaigned aggressively for parliamentary reform and Catholic rights, and were a major force behind the legislative victories on these fronts toward the end of the eighteenth century. By the mid 1790s the war with France had emboldened the United Irishmen to make ever more daring demands, and with the country abuzz with rebellion, the Ascendancy seemed in peril. In the summer of 1795, armed bands of Catholics and Protestants skirmished in County Armagh in what became known as the Battle of the Diamond; in the wake of the battle, the Orange Society was formed to protect the interests of Protestants and the Crown in Ireland. Initially a secret society, the Orange Order quickly spread throughout Ireland and into England, and today Orange lodges can be found in most English-speaking countries.

More than two centuries later, the Orange Order remains a controversial body. Often censured for propagating sectarian differences, the Orangemen continue to hold their colorful parades each twelfth of July to commemorate William's victory over the papists, sometimes marching through predominantly Catholic neighborhoods, though in the Republic the parades usually run their course without controversy. In Northern Ireland the Orange Order was (until quite recently) intrinsic to the Ulster Unionist Party, which controlled the provincial government in the north until 1972.

then turned the novel into a play, which was a huge success at London's Adelphi Theatre. Lover wrote a few more novels after this, but with age he was drawn to the stage above all else, taking his show *Irish Evenings*—comprised of light Irish folktales, songs, and music—to venues as far away as America.

WILLIAM CARLETON AND CHARLES MATURIN

If it is true that Lover and Lever lacked sincerity and realism, and Maria Edgeworth was sincere but her fiction lacked realism, then William Carleton had all the tools for realism but struggled to be taken as being sincere. He gives the most complete picture of the lives of Irish peasants in a half-century of active writing, but was never able to shed his reputation as a man of compromised integrity. This is partly because he was prone to drink and partly because he was a womanizer, but mostly because finances frequently forced him to write for whomever would pay him to do so. Often these were Protestant publishers who wanted Carleton, who had abandoned his training as a Catholic priest, to write anti-Catholic propaganda. Simple economics had him at their mercy, and his reputation for bigotry never went away, even though Carleton is clearly on the side of Catholics in some of his best and most widely-read books. Perhaps the vilification he endured during his life and since his death would not have been so severe had his pen been not so effective.

Carleton was born a poor Catholic peasant in County Tyrone—the youngest of fourteen children, six of whom died before Carleton was born. Carleton's father, like his grandfather, was a tenant farmer. His parents lacked education, though his father spoke English and Irish fluently and had an illimitable memory. He was able to recite the entire Bible, could call up a passage by the number of its chapter and verse, and, most famously, carried with him so many tales, poems, and other Irish folklore that Carleton claimed he never heard a new one for the rest of his life. Everywhere in his autobiography, which was incomplete at Carleton's death, he laments the poor state of education in Ireland, and he must have wondered what his parents might have become had laws not forbidden the education of the Catholic populace. Carleton's own success in school had him earmarked for the priesthood, but as he grew older he began to have difficulty with some of the dogma of the Roman Catholic Church. With a sense of adventure inspired by a copy of *Gil Blas* and a good knowledge of classical literature, he made his way for Dublin in 1818.

Carleton figured his best chance at making a living was as a teacher, though his autobiography, in laying out the details of his early years in the city, shows him often struggling just to find food, let alone a job. Hilarious at times and at times unfathomable, he recounts both terribly bad luck and the fantastic charity of strangers. Having arrived in Dublin on foot at night, he found a room for rent on Dirty Lane (the name was changed to Bridgefoot Street in Carleton's lifetime). But when the house's proprietors discovered the little money he had they took him for an indigent, and threatened to throw him out in the middle of the night. After some begging they allowed him to sleep in the basement, in which, thanks to the institution of the Poor Laws in Dublin that kept the destitute out of the parks and off the street, droves of beggars, drunks, derelicts, and invalids slept in straw beds.

> The cellar was very spacious: I should think that the entrance into Dante's Inferno was paradise compared with it. I know and have known Dublin now for about half a century, better probably than any other man in it. I have lived in Liberty and in every close and outlet in [Dublin], driven by poverty to the most wretched of localities, and I must confess that the scene which burst upon me that night stands beyond anything the highest flight of my imagination could have conceived without my having an opportunity of seeing it. (Carleton, *The Autobiography of William Carleton* 163–64)

The wretched people, with their infirmities such as missing limbs and scrofulous neck swellings, composed such a terrible scene that it "made me reflect upon the degree of perverted talent and ingenuity that must have been necessary to sustain such a mighty mass of imposture" (164). Carleton guesses there were about two dozen of these cellar dwellings in the city, which came under scrutiny after the cholera outbreak in 1832. His estimate was conservative: between 1841 and 1857, 2205 such cellar dwellings were closed in Dublin, and several dozen were in use as late as 1873. It is no wonder Carleton took any job or charity available.

Without money or friends, Carleton bounced all around Dublin. When on Castle Street he bursts into tears at his complete poverty in a shoemaker's shop run by a man of the same name, the owner gives him five shillings. He lived at no. 4 Moore Street, where he met a lamebrained tailor who enlisted Carleton's help in writing his memoirs. The man offered to pay for Carleton's room and board in exchange for his services, but when, after more than a month, the time came to settle the bill, the tailor had vanished, forcing Carleton to do the same. At his next lodgings in Mary's Lane he attracted the attentions of the landlady (Carleton was, by all accounts, a handsome, athletic man) whom he had to blackmail to avoid paying a monstrous bill when he told her he was leaving. He stayed in a room adjoining a circulating library on Francis Street next, which he enjoyed thoroughly, reading sometimes for sixteen hours a day, most of it smut. "[S]uch a mass of obscenity and profligacy was ... never put together. How the booksellers were found to publish the books is difficult to say, or how they escaped prosecution" (176–177).

At length Carleton did manage to secure several positions tutoring and teaching, and when he had a little money he took advantage of Dublin's possibilities. He went to concerts and plays, frequenting the Crow Street theatre built by the actor Spranger Barry in 1758, and the Theatre Royal in Hawkins Street—neither has survived. A chance meeting with the deputy librarian of Marsh's Library, which he describes as "almost unknown," made him a regular patron there. "This was the first public library I had ever seen," he writes, "and I wondered at the time how such an incredible number of books could be read, or, which comes to much about the same thing, how a sufficient number of scholars could be found to read them" (189).

One of the few patrons in the underexploited library was the gothic novelist Charles Maturin, who wrote several of his books there. Maturin was born in Dublin to a Huguenot family, of the many immigrating to the city after the Edict of Fontainebleau was issued in 1685. He studied for a clerical career at Trinity College, and was ordained in the Church of Ireland after graduating in 1800. By 1805 he had married and begun a family. He won the curacy of St. Peter's, Aungier Street, but like Swift, he would never rise higher in the Church. Short on money, Maturin began tutoring students to prepare them for the university and started to write fiction. He self-published *Fatal Revenge*, a gothic tale which was read by almost no one, in 1807, and finished *The Wild Irish Boy* for 1808, a knockoff of Lady Sydney Owenson Morgan's *The Wild Irish Girl*, published just a year earlier. His fortune changed when he discovered that Sir Walter Scott was the author of an anonymous, positive review of *Fatal Revenge*. The ensuing correspondence between the two writers gave Maturin confidence and connections, and Maturin was desperate for both: his father had lost his job as a road inspector for the Irish General Post Office in Dublin in 1809, and his brother declared bankruptcy in 1813. Maturin sent his play *Bertram* to Scott, who recommended it to Byron, who had it staged in London in 1816. This, finally, was lucrative, earning Maturin £1000, but most of the money went to pay his brother's debts.

Despite his ongoing money problems, Maturin was famous enough to be recognized by Carleton in Marsh's Library, and famous enough that Carleton knew where he lived, at no. 37 York Street. The passage in Carleton's autobiography where he decides to pay a visit to the spooky Maturin, to see "what a man of genius could be like," is certainly tongue-in-cheek. He describes the gothic novelist in slippers and a huge brown coat, dressed like a charity case. "At that time I had read so little of the habits or personal appearance of men of genius, that I knew not what inference to draw from his" (*Autobiography of William Carleton* 190). In truth, Maturin's eccentricities were well-known in Dublin even before Carleton met the man, and by the time Carleton wrote of the encounter it may be said that he was known for little else but his eccentricities. For one, the cleric seemed to be unable to stop dancing, which he did during the day (hiding behind the curtains of his York Street house) and late into the night. His dress varied greatly, from the rags Carelton encountered to the most fanciful pantaloons. He liked to write in company, so to signal to those around him that he was working he would paste a wafer to his forehead. If he found himself intrigued by their conversation, he glued his mouth shut with wheat paste. He was vain and somewhat needy, and he wrote as much for fame as he did for money. But in the course of trying to find a literary register that worked out his own peculiar sentiments—which happened to be the already waning gothic novel—he wound up producing some of the best examples in that genre.

Not all Maturin's works can be properly called gothic—especially the two nationalist books he wrote after the initial failure of *Fatal Revenge*—but even his more realistic fiction maintains bleak and sublime tones. On the coattails of his successful play *Bertram*, he produced *Women, or Pour et Contre*, in a conscious effort to write with a greater degree of realism. But still Maturin opens the novel in a deserted Phoenix Park, with the novel's hero De Courcy alone, on foot, somewhat lost, making his way to the city at night.

> It was past seven when he reached the outskirts of Dublin, and, mistaking a direction given him at the entrance of Barrack-street, he crossed into the north-circular road, and, with the murmur and the lights of the city still before him, and

appearing almost round him, he reached the Canal Bridge.
He was alone; as he crossed it, he was startled by the cries of a
female voice, piercing, but suddenly stopped;—he rushed
forward,—a carriage thundering over the bridge passed him
rapidly, and in a few moments the rolling of the wheels at a
distance, as it pursued the way to the country, was the only
sound to be heard. (Maturin, *Women, or Pour et Contre* 10)

The horror of the dark, speeding carriage, the screams of a girl
in distress, and a man urging the driver on "with frightful
imprecations" continues in an old cottage inhabited by a mad
hag (where De Courcy rescues the girl), but the Gothicism ends
there. Despite this slight imbalance, the book sold reasonably
well.

Maturin is probably best known today either for *Melmoth the
Wanderer*, his Gothic masterpiece, or for being Oscar Wilde's
grand-uncle. When Wilde, having served time in London's Old
Bailey on a sodomy charge, exiled himself to France, the alias he
took was Sebastian Melmoth, a name carefully borrowed from
Maturin's Faustian figure. *Melmoth the Wanderer* is a frame
story, sometimes three and four levels deep. The main narrative
centers on a Trinity College student, John Melmoth, who gets
an old manuscript from his uncle, who is dying of fright. From
his uncle and the manuscript, John discovers that his ancestor
(the Wanderer) sold his soul to the Devil in exchange for
immortality, and, now over one hundred-fifty years old, he
travels the world, tormenting men to do the same. Nobody ever
takes Melmoth's bargain, no matter how terrible their situation.
Maturin's intent is to play out one of his sermons, the crux of
which he quotes in the book's preface:

At this moment is there one of us present, however we may
have departed from the Lord, disobeyed his will, and disre-
garded his word—is there one of us who would, at this
moment, accept all that man could bestow, or earth afford,
to resign the hope of his salvation?—No, there is not one—

not such a fool on earth, were the enemy of mankind to tra-
verse it with the offer! (Maturin, *Melmoth the Wanderer*
ix–x)

While a noble cause, this message is lost in the novel's entertaining horror (on the one hand) and its depictions of human
cruelty (on the other). Maturin died just four years after the
publication of *Melmoth*, and though it enjoyed immediate success, the novel and Maturin disappeared into obscurity. It was
not published again until 1894, when Oscar Wilde wrote a new
preface to the book. Still in print today, it remains a favorite of
Gothic enthusiasts as a classic of the form.

Carleton still had not published when Maturin died in 1824.
But beginning in 1828, his essays and stories became regular
fixtures in Dublin's magazines. *The Lough Derg Pilgrim*, his first
published work, was written at the invitation of Caesar Otway,
whose *Christian Examiner* was rank with anti-Catholic misan-
thropy. Even after he left the Church, Carleton claims to have
held no animosity towards Catholics or the priesthood. This is
probably true, though it was certainly not apparent in his work.
Other contributions appeared in *Family Magazine, Dublin University Magazine*, and *The Nation*. The last of these was the
vehicle of Thomas Davis and the nationalist Young Irelanders,
though, like the indifference behind his "anti-Roman" pieces for
the *Christian Examiner*, Carleton never developed any nationalist opinions, or if he did he never made them public.

In 1830 the Dublin publisher Brooke put out two volumes
of Carleton's *Traits and Stories of the Irish Peasantry*. By 1834
selections from his stories in Otway's magazine were bound and
reprinted as *Tales of Ireland*. An illustrated compendium of
Traits and Stories appeared in 1842, with characters so exact it
was practically treated as an anthropological document. Karl
Marx became infatuated with the first volume, writing to
Engels in 1879 that the author lacked any talent for style, but
that "his originality lies in the truth of his descriptions. As the
son of an Irish peasant he knows his subject better than the

Levers and Lovers" (*www.marxists.org/archive/marx/ works/1879/letters/79_08_14.htm*). *Traits and Stories* was in its eleventh edition by 1876. In 1845 he published his first novel, *Valentine McClutchy*, a heavy satire on the actions of the Orange Society, who terrorized Carleton's family on one occasion when he was a boy, stabbing his sister with a bayonet in the middle of the night. (Better known as the Orangemen, this Protestant organization sprang up in response to legislation favoring Catholics in the late eighteenth century, becoming a secret society in 1795—with lodges even in England—intent on securing Protestant interests.) The book is very much on the side of the Irish Catholics, its eviction scene especially heart-wrenching.

The year *Valentine McClutchy* appeared, the Great Famine officially took hold in Ireland. Careful observers had noted the possibility for disaster in Ireland's agricultural sector: antiquarian farming methods, the uneducated, booming population working tiny plots for subsistence only, completely dependent on one crop—the potato—tied to the markets of an industrializing England—all conspired to make the worst of a new fungus afflicting the potato plant in the wet Irish weather. Many in the country had lived at the edge of starvation before the potato crop failed. The numbers are thusly preposterous: more than a million died from starvation or diseases catalyzed by malnutrition; more than a million left the country. Ireland's population decreased by 1.8 million between 1847 and 1851 alone, and continued to decline into the twentieth century.

Carleton wrote of the famine in *The Black Prophet*, which he penned while it still raged in the countryside, "in a season of such unparalleled scarcity and destitution" (Carleton, *The Black Prophet* iii). His purposes are made clear in the preface: to present the gritty details of the famine "to awaken those who legislate for us into something like a humane perception of a calamity that has been almost perennial in our country" (iii), and to present an account as good as history for those with enough distance to forget the catastrophe:

[Since] the memory of our Legislature is as faithless on such a subject as that of the most heartless individual among us, the author deemed it an act of public usefulness to his countrymen, to record in the following pages such an authentic history of those deadly periods of famine to which they have been so frequently subject, as could be relied upon with confidence by all who might feel an interest in placing them beyond the reach of this terrible scourge. (iv)

The book is dedicated to the Prime Minister, Russell, who chose to adhere to laissez-faire economics rather than purchase food for the starving, like his predecessor Peel. Claims that this was a conscious effort to exterminate the country's undesirables have been proven false.

Neither *Valentine McClutchy* nor *The Black Prophet* was as successful as *Willy Reilly and His Dear Colleen Brown*, which went through more than fifty editions. Set in the days of the Penal Laws and based on the popular street ballad of the same name, it is not his best work. The fecundity of Carleton's pen lasted as long as he did; the pages of his autobiography—his last work—is virile, funny, and detailed as anything else, however abrupt its end. From about 1853 to 1855 he lived in a small home in the North Dublin suburb of Marino, at no. 3 Marino Terrace, north of Fairview Park. Today, Carleton Road in that neighborhood is named in his honor. He spent his remaining years in a house at no. 2 Rathgar Avenue in Woodville, South Dublin, where he died in 1869. Benedict Kiely, Carleton's adoring biographer, provides this eulogy while visiting his grave in Mount Jerome cemetery:

Standing there under the dark cool chestnut trees I find it always difficult to realise that the body laid in the earth was old and feeble and heavily bearded. When the wind moves the long leaves and when a bird, venturing down into the city, sings suddenly from the branches, down in the earth the heart that responds must still be young and eager, and the body the strong body of a boy who idles forever in a green valley with the lost people of Ireland. (Kiely 197)

Celtic Revivalists before the turn of the next century gave Carleton all the credit they could muster. Yeats posits in his introduction to 1889's *Stories from Carleton* that he was "the great novelist of Ireland, by right of the most Celtic eyes that ever gazed from under the brows of story-teller," (Carleton, *Stories from Carleton* xvi).

JOSEPH SHERIDAN LE FANU

Of the Dublin authors who may be credited with establishing the Irish novel in the English language, horror writer Joseph Sheridan Le Fanu lived the latest—though not quite long enough to see the work of the scholars of the Celtic Revival (Ferguson, Petrie, and others), who had begun their work in Le Fanu's lifetime, reflected in the literature of Yeats, Moore, Gregory, and Russell. From the Protestant middle class, he was probably the last of the major Irish novelists to cling to the shreds of Ascendancy privilege; the later Victorians, like Wilde and Stoker, simply went to England to please the English, and much of the Irish literature after that is married to nationalism. But Le Fanu haunted Dublin for all his days as an active writer, and in fact seldom left his house in Merrion Square, prompting Dubliners to refer to the spooky author as the "Invisible Prince."

Like Charles Maturin, Sheridan was from Huguenot stock. His ancestors came to Ireland after the revocation of the Edict of Nantes drove hordes of Protestants from France. Hardly simple weavers, though, the Le Fanus served under William III in his Irish campaigns against James and the Catholics, for which they were rewarded handsomely. One William Le Fanu became a large property holder in Dublin. His son, Joseph Le Fanu, married Richard Brinsley Sheridan's sister Alicia. Thomas Philip Le Fanu was produced from this match in 1784; he became a student of Theology at Trinity College, took orders, and became the curate of St. Mary's Church, Dublin. In 1814, his wife Emma had a son, Joseph Sheridan Le Fanu, born in North Dublin at 45 Dominick Street. Preferment came quickly for Thomas, and the next year the family moved to a house near Phoenix Park, closer to the Royal Hibernian Military School (St. Mary's Chest Hospital today) where he was named chaplain. Joseph thusly spent his first twelve years with the forests, gardens, and fields of Phoenix Park as his playground, which has changed little (except the zoo, which was added in 1830) since Le Fanu's boyhood there. Earlier in the history of Dublin the park had been the private hunting grounds of the nobility, but its 1800 wild acres did not survive the Georgian interests of Lord Chesterfield, who planted the gardens and thinned the trees into copses to suit his tastes. He also erected the Phoenix column, depicting a phoenix rising from its ashes, near the little spring that waters the park. The subject of the column only reinforces the corruption of the Irish language that gives Phoenix Park its name. In Irish, the place was called *Fionn uisg*, a homophone of *phoenix* that means "clear water" (i.e. the spring). The name stuck. When Lord Chesterfield made the park public it became—like so many metropolitan green spaces—a venue for robbers and, most frequently at dawn—duels.

Surprisingly, the twelve-year-old Joseph was not disappointed to leave such a place of adventure when, in 1826, his father was named rector of Abington in County Limerick. There, thanks to the negligence of a tutor too often distracted by fly-fishing to care about the instruction of Le Fanu and his brother, the young man enjoyed unfettered access to his father's estimable library. He returned to Dublin in 1832 to attend Trinity College, where he read classics and was active in the College Historical Society. Despite an introverted youth, Le Fanu seemed set for a career in politics when he took his degree in 1837, but when *The Ghost and the Bonesetter*, his first short story, was published in the *Dublin University Magazine* with almost a dozen more to follow, he decided his future lay in letters, not law.

To this end, Le Fanu bought several Dublin publications beginning in the 1840s, including the *Warder*, the *Protestant Guardian*, and shares in the *Statesman* and others—all colored with Protestant and Tory views. He married Susanna Bennett in 1843, the family settling at 15 Warrington Place until they inherited the home at 18 Merrion Square (it still stands, now no. 70) in 1851.

After lengthy and severe bouts of depression, Susanna died in 1858, when she was just thirty-four years old. Le Fanu had had slight success with a few historical novels, and published some ghost stories in the *Dublin University Magazine*, but his writing dried up after 1853. With four young children to care for, substantial debt, a nanny to pay, and considerable grief, Le Fanu turned to fiction for income. He bought the *Dublin University Magazine* in 1863 and started to fill its pages with his own work. The first of his novels to be published serially in this space was *The House by the Churchyard*, a dark but comical murder mystery set in Chapelizod in the previous century. Seven more novels appeared in the next six years, all printed initially in the triple-decker, as the three-part serial was called. Le Fanu abandoned this format at last with his collection of short stories *In a Glass Darkly*, published just a year before his death.

Le Fanu remained somewhat sociable through most of the 1860s, receiving his friend Charles Lever, among others, in Merrion Square, but from the late 60s to his death he almost never left home and turned away all visitors. He wrote his ghastly tales in bed by candlelight, usually after midnight and before dawn. When he left home it was in the faint light of the evening, combing Dublin's bookstores for macabre and supernatural material. He died of a heart attack, nightmare-plagued and alone, in 1873.

CHAPTER FIVE

Remembering a Nation

It was while O'Connell's Repeal Association was in full swing, with the dew still drying off Catholic Emancipation and the first editions of William Carleton's *Traits and Stories of the Irish Peasantry* just off the presses, that the literature of Ireland's past was met with genuine scholarship. Ferguson and Petrie, and his associates O'Donovan and O'Curry, were beginning their careful translations of Irish literature around 1830, and yet these and other scholars might have attracted little attention and no patronage if it hadn't been for the forgeries of James MacPherson some seventy years earlier.

Published in 1761, MacPherson's *Ossian*, a collection of supposed translations of Scots Gaelic manuscripts by the legendary poet of the same name, raged through a literate England in the clutches of Sensibility. Claiming to have found the ancient texts on a tour of the Scottish highlands, MacPherson discovered an audience eager for antiquities. Some ears pricked up when MacPherson failed to reveal his manuscripts to scholars, but on the whole his *Ossian* and the later *Temora* survived the century at face value. Gaelic scholars were later able to point out the many anachronisms (linguistic and otherwise) in MacPherson's work, though, ironically, it was in a large part due to MacPherson's success and popularity that Gaelic scholarship got off the ground.

Questions of *Ossian*'s authenticity were raised as early as 1766. They persisted within the institution of the Royal Irish Academy, founded in 1785 as an apparatus of the Ascendancy to provide a historical legitimacy to Protestant aristocrats whose ancestors had married into prominent Irish families. The foundation of the RIA marks the beginning of unprecedented interest on the part of the Anglo-Irish in the history of a culture it had formerly ignored or willfully denigrated. And though this early period in Gaelic historiography was full of risible theories—many of the foremost scholars, for instance, posited a connection between ancient Irish and Phoencian—it exacted enough interest for more careful hands to take up the discovery and translation of ancient Irish literature. After a dip in interest in the years following the Act of Union, Irish antiquarianism

Oisín (Ossian)

Supposed son of Finn Mac Cumhaill (MacCool), Oisín , whose name means little dear, is the legendary warrior-bard who sang of Finn's exploits with his militia, the Fianna Éirann. Set in the third century, the poems became known as Fenian or Ossianic cycles and though the tales were less violent than those of the previous period, the Ulaid Cycle, they were often filled with battles and adventures. Two of the great tales from this cycle are *The Pursuit of Diarmuid and Grainne* and *Oisín in Tir na nOg*. *Oisín in Tir na nOg* is the tale of how Oisín falls in love with the fairy Niamh and leaves for the island of *Tir na nOg*. After what he believes is three years, he returns to find that 300 years have passed. He is warned by Niamh not to dismount or else he will become old and withered, but while helping some men load a stone into a wagon, he falls to the ground and becomes old.

was taken up by Catholics and Protestants alike. Often motivated for different reasons, these scholars began to unearth a culture that most of the world had no knowledge of. For autochthonous, downtrodden Irish Catholics, it inspired a sense of pride in an older culture of kings and their bards; for the Protestant Anglo-Irish, it lent new legitimacy to their own Irishness; and for the English it garnered a new sentiment for Ireland and its romantic history.

THOMAS MOORE

Thomas Moore was gilding this lily. Many have credited the musical poet for instilling in the English a new fascination with the Irish, and it is true that his Irish airs repackaged with English words were the haute couture of London's salons in the early nineteenth century. Later, more purist critics dubbed Moore a sort of sell-out, who spoon-fed Irish poetry to the rest of Great Britain at the expense of Irish poetry; but only in the strictest nationalist context is this a failing. Even in the first series of Moore's *Irish Melodies* (1808) there are veiled references to the death of Robert Emmet, that star-crossed patriot who was executed after the rising of 1803, with whom Moore was friendly. A Catholic himself, he supported Emancipation, especially in his satiric novel *Memoirs of Captain Rock.* Yet in part because of his closeness to the English aristocracy (he dedicated his *Odes of Anachreon* to the Prince Regent in 1800), in part because he did not support O'Connell's movement to repeal, and in part because "he was an Englishman's idea of what an Irishman should be," as J.B. Priestly wrote in the introduction to Moore's diary (ix), Moore and his work did not fare well in the combustible nationalist climate of the Irish famine and its aftermath. Yet there is no such thing as bad publicity, and Moore took his sentimental vision of Ireland across the sea and into the very drawing-rooms of England.

Moore was born the son of a grocer and wine merchant at 12 Aungier Street in 1779, where a small plaque on the building marks the place of his birth, today, ironically, a jazz club. Both his parents, being Catholic, were sympathetic to nationalist causes. He was a good student, and after attending Samuel Whyte's Academy (79 Grafton Street), alma mater of R.B. Sheridan, he became one of the first students to enjoy the 1793 easing of restrictions that had barred Catholics from entering Trinity College. There he met Emmet, debated in the Historical Society, flirted with the United Irishmen, and became familiar with Edward Bunting's recent *General Collection of Ancient Irish Music* (1796). After graduation he removed to London to study law, and the early success of *Odes of Anachreon* won him a sinecure in Bermuda. *Irish Melodies*, many set to Bunting's airs, were published in London by J. Power (who conceived the idea in the first place) beginning in 1808. These made Moore famous early, and he continued to contribute to the series through 1834. His songs "'Tis the Last Rose of Summer" and "Meeting of the Waters," originally published in *Irish Melodies*, are recognizable today. He became friends with Byron and Sir Walter Scott, and earned a huge advance (£3,000) for his huge poem *Lalla Rookh* (1817), styled Oriental on Byron's advice. The story concerns a princess traveling from Delhi to Kashmir, where she is to marry the king of Bucharia. Along the way she is entertained with stories from the young poet Feramorz, with whom she falls in love. The poem took Moore four years to write, and when finished, struck its readers with its heavy, Oriental flavor, even impressing those in the Middle East with its detail. Ostensible in *Lalla Rookh* was the Irish-English allegory in one of its main narratives, in which the Persian Fire-Worshippers struggle against the oppressive Muslims, and the love story of Hafed and Hinda was easily recognized as a reference to Moore's friend, Robert Emmet, and his secret fiancée Sarah Curran. The book saw twenty editions before Moore's death in 1852.

The belated regard Moore earned in Ireland evidences his primarily British audience. "Written for the English drawing-room," wrote Moore's biographer L.A.G. Strong, "the *Melodies* took a long time to reach the people of Ireland" (Strong 138).

On one trip to his hometown in 1830 Moore had a startling revelation, recorded in his diary on September 14:

> Have observed (what I should not have believed had I not witnessed it) that the Irish are much colder auditors (to *my* singing, at least) than the English. Nothing like the same *empressement*, the crowding towards the pianoforte, the eagerness for more which I am accustomed to in most English companies. This may be, perhaps, from my being made so much a *lion* here, or from some notion of good breeding and finery, some idea probably that it is more fashionable and *English* not to be moved. From whatever reason it may proceed, it is the last thing I should have expected. (Moore 151–152)

It did not help that Moore never again lived in Dublin after he left. He did all his work in London, or on the Continent, where he was forced to live for a time to pay off a bad debt. The proxy he had hired to perform his duties in Bermuda was caught in an embezzlement scheme, incurring a liability that belonged ultimately to Moore. In Paris he wrote constantly to come up with the money. He saw Byron, who entrusted Moore with his memoirs, which after much hand-wringing and squabbles with Byron's friends and family he decided to burn out of respect to Lady Byron. Finally settling the debt, Moore moved back to England in 1822.

In later life Moore had success in prose, writing several fine biographies, one, even, of the rebel Lord Edward Fitzgerald, at the risk of offending his English patrons. In consideration of this and of the overall sentiment Moore drew from the English for the Irish, it is only in the volatile circumstances of mid-century Ireland that his gains toward an Irish literature could be deigned shortcoming. Thomas Davis, at the center of this volatility, criticized Moore in his weekly, the *Nation*, calling even his political songs "too despondent or weak to content a people marching to independence as proudly as if they had never been slaves" (Davis 206). As the new century approached, agitation for an Irish nation (and an Irish national literature) increased, and Moore was relegated to the fringes of Irish literary history, a man with no Irish background or the will to acquire one. Yeats omitted Moore from his survey of *Popular Ballad Poetry of Ireland*, writing that he, and Lover and Lever, "were never poets of the people."

> Moore lived in the drawing-rooms, and still finds his audience therein. Lever and Lover, kept apart by opinion from the body of the nation, wrote ever with one eye on London. They never wrote for the people, and neither have they ever, therefore, in prose or verse, written faithfully of the people. Ireland was a metaphor to Moore, to Lever and Lover a merry harlequin, sometimes even pathetic, to be patted and pitied and laughed at so long as he said "your honour," and presumed in nowise to be considered a serious or tragic person. (Yeats, *Uncollected Prose* 161–162)

Despite shifting attitudes, Moore is still generally considered Ireland's national poet, his statue in College Green erected just six years after his death, in 1857. Leopold Bloom walks underneath "Tommy Moore's roguish finger" in *Ulysses*, recording the statue's laughable placement. "They did it right to put him up over a urinal: meeting of the waters" (Joyce, *Ulysses* 133), alluding to Moore's famous Irish air. The urinal has since been removed.

THOMAS DAVIS
Nearby, the statue of Moore's contemporary Thomas Davis occupies the former site of that much-defaced equestrian statue of William III. Writ large on the pedestal are the years of Davis's short life: he was a month shy of his thirty-first birthday when struck down by a fever. It was a ferocious though not fatal blow to the movement he led, the Young Irelanders, who went on to stage the rebellion of 1848 and failed.

As a poet, Davis was mediocre; his contribution to Irish literature consists materially of a few national ballads. Much more important to literary history is Davis's commitment to cultivating Irish literature in the first place, one of the many causes he took up in the weekly Dublin newspaper, the *Nation*, where most of his work was published.

Thomas Davis's father was already dead a month before his youngest son was born in County Cork, 1814. He had been a doctor in the British Army, from Welsh ancestry long settled in Ireland. Davis's mother, Mary Atkins, was of a Protestant family that came to Ireland with Cromwell. The details of how Davis developed his nationalist opinions amidst a family so entrenched on the side of the English are not known, but given his comments and his zealous support of mixed education, over which he split with O'Connell's group, we can surmise he formed his opinions in Dublin's schools. Davis's mother moved the family to Dublin in 1818, when he was four, and he first attended the mixed seminary of Mr. Mungan on Lower Mount Street. He later claimed in his education debates with Daniel O'Connell that knowing classmates of different creed and backgrounds at the mixed school inspired his love for all his countrymen. From the time the Davis family came to Dublin until Thomas was fifteen they lived in a house on Warrington Place, but in 1830 they moved to Lower Baggot Street, now no. 67, marked today by a small plaque. Davis lived in this house with his mother, brothers, and sister until he died there from a relapse of scarlet fever in 1845.

At seventeen Davis entered Trinity College, where he had a reputation for avid reading but little else. He took a B.A. in 1836, and after some time spent in London finishing his studies in law, he came back to Dublin, becoming a member of the Dublin Historical Society. To this group he spoke in 1838, pleading for the study of Irish history, but the real beginning of Davis's public life was an 1840 speech to the Trinity College Historical Society, in which he denounced the antiquated curriculum of the University, and concluded by imploring his

audience—fresh, mostly Protestant Trinity College graduates—
to use their minds, their knowledge, and their future positions
of power in the service of their country. That Davis should
make this address in the veritable bastion of the Ascendancy
that was Trinity College is indicative of his overall vision for Ireland. Where Daniel O'Connell's fights for Emancipation and
Repeal were Catholic concerns in opposition to not only England, but, often enough, Irish Protestants, Davis sought to unite
Catholic and Protestant factions, and for the first time, to build
an Irish republic.

It was the next year, in 1841, that Davis and his Catholic
friend John Blake Dillon met the journalist Charles Gavin
Duffy, editor of a Catholic journal in Belfast. The three met
again at the Four Courts Building the following spring, and,
after a famous walk through Phoenix Park, they laid their plans
for the weekly *Nation*. In the public advertisement for their
paper they wrote their reason for publishing a liberal paper in
Dublin, when more than a few already existed:

> Nationality is their first great object—a Nationality which
> will not only raise our people from their poverty, by securing
> to them the blessings of a DOMESTIC LEGISLATION,
> but inflame and purify them with a lofty and heroic love of
> country,—a Nationality of the spirit as well as the letter;—a
> Nationality which may come to be stamped upon our man-
> ners, our literature, and our deeds,—a Nationality which
> may embrace Protestant, Catholic, and Dissenter,—Milesian
> and Cromwellian,—the Irishman of a hundred generations
> and the stranger who is within out gates;—not a Nationality
> which would prelude civil war; but which would establish
> internal union and external independence;—a Nationality
> which would be recognized by the world, and sanctified by
> wisdom, virtue, and prudence. (Mulvey 63–64)

Davis was the paper's main contributor, Duffy the editor, and
Dillon an early planner but later a silent influence. All three

were under the age of thirty, and the new political movement they spearheaded was rightly dubbed (but not by them) the Young Irelanders. Davis wrote upwards of 200 essays and editorials the first year alone, but even Duffy sometimes wrote for the paper. Besides the essays, the *Nation* printed book reviews, news from around the world, and, of course poetry. To fill space Duffy asked Davis to write "national ballads" for the paper. Duffy later wrote that:

> Davis assured me he had never published a verse, though like most men of culture in the process of self-eduation he had written and destroyed reams of paper covered with rhymes. Within a fortnight he brought me the "Death of Owen Roe" ... and week after week, for three years, he poured out songs as spontaneously as a bird. (Duffy 69)

Davis came to contribute more than 80 poems to the *Nation,* including ballads still sung—*A Nation Once Again* and *The West's Asleep,* for instance, and some good historical poems—*Fontenoy,* among others—but his strong suit was his often fiery essays. The paper was a huge success, some estimates claiming as many as 250,000 readers. Davis's death in 1845 prompted Duffy to organize a public funeral with a long procession from Davis's deathbed on Baggot Street to the site of his burial in Mount St. Jerome cemetery, where a large sculpture marks his grave.

Davis was not the only poet writing in the *Nation.* Speranza (Lady Wilde), though raised a Unionist, flirted with the Young Irelanders for a time, writing some of the *Nation's* most revolutionary poetry. She was not tried for treason as other contributors for the paper were after the abortive rising of 1848, probably due to her status. Duffy, on the other hand, was jailed in Newgate, but legal wizardry earned acquittals and delays, keeping him mostly out of prison. (He emigrated in 1855, began a long career in Australian politics, and was knighted in 1873.) John Keegan Casey wrote several lyrics for the paper, and Thomas

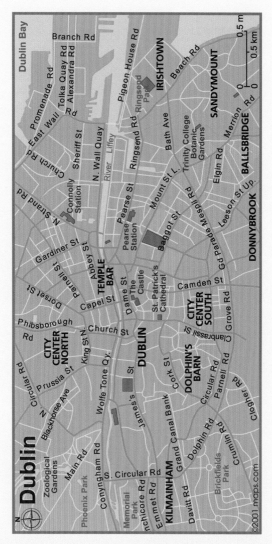

■ Dublin's modern city construction, completed in the sixteenth century, centers around Dublin Castle which held the offices of the British viceroy of Ireland. The city's wide avenues and large squares were once Celtic routes, remodeled by the Vikings and again by Georgian influence during the eighteenth century. Dublin lies in the flat valley of the Liffey River, which cuts through the city east to west, making the city Ireland's most prominent seaport.

■ Oliver Cromwell, born in 1599, was a staunch Calvinist and held a seat in England's House of Commons before rising to the title Lord Protector. Cromwell strove to eradicate Royalists and Catholics from Ireland, but instead left the country in economic disaster.

■ With history dating back to St. Patrick's visit to Ireland in 432, St. Patrick's Cathedral is the largest church in Ireland. Patrick, according to tradition, baptized converts in the park that now lies adjacent to the cathedral. In order to celebrate this event, a small wooden church was built.

■ Jonathan Swift, famous for *Gulliver's Travels* (1726), is a renowned Irish poet, satirist, political activist, and pamphleteer. Swift was born in Dublin and became active in the Church, traveling between Ireland and England. In response to Ireland's state of economy, Swift wrote the satire *A Modest Proposal* (1729), outlining the use of babies to feed the masses.

■ Trinity College's Long Room boasts over 4 million in book stock, the oldest of the college's volumes, and the prestige of being the oldest library in Ireland. Built between 1712 and 1732 by Thomas Burgh, the library now serves the patrons of Trinity College. Art is displayed in the Long Room including a bust of Jonathan Swift.

■ Trinity College, Dublin, was founded by Queen Elizabeth I in 1592 and is the only constituent college of the University of Dublin, Ireland's oldest college. Trinity sprawls over 47 acres in College Green, across from the former Irish Houses of Parliament in Dublin.

■ Born in Ireland and educated at Trinity College, Oscar Wilde became known for his acerbic wit as well as for his eccentric and flamboyant lifestyle. Wilde later moved to London where he became a literary success and was eventually tried for indecency.

■ George Bernard Shaw, a Dublin native, moved to London in 1876 where he became a playwright, critic, social spokesman, and woman's rights activist. Shaw was awarded the Nobel Prize in Literature in 1925; although he accepted the honor, he declined the monetary award.

■ William Butler Yeats studied at the Metropolitan School of Art in Dublin. Yeats's poetry centered around the bitter folklore of his Irish ancestry. His poetry ranges from lush romanticism to intellectual poetry, reflecting the styles of his peers at that particular time. Yeats is also noted for his fascination with the supernatural, reincarnation, speaking with the dead, and Oriental mysticism.

■ One of Dublin's most famous writers, James Joyce revolutionized literature with his 'stream of consciousness' technique and symbolic parallels. Facing publication rejection, misunderstanding from critics, and public scrutiny, Joyce became a writing nomad in 1902 although his writing was heavily influenced by his Irish heritage.

■ Mounted on the door of no. 7 Eccles Street in Dublin is a framed document recounting the history of the door. The residency is noted as the home of Leopold Bloom in James Joyce's *Ulysses*. The James Joyce Center houses the door as part of its exhibit.

■ Born on Good Friday, the thirteenth in 1906, Samuel Beckett became Ireland's most famous modern absurdist playwright. Suffering from chronic loneliness, Beckett traveled extensively, befriending James Joyce in Paris. Beckett's plays focus on the struggles against meaninglessness and with human suffering and survival, often reflecting a commedia dell'arte style. Beckett's play *Waiting for Godot* is one of the most noted of the Theatre of the Absurd.

D'Arcy McGee provided a number of nationalist poems. But James Clarence Mangan was the most talented poet to write for the periodical, and likely the most talented poet of the time.

JAMES CLARENCE MANGAN

This is not to suggest that Mangan was a nationalist—certainly not one germane to Davis and Duffy. In fact, the array of periodicals in which we find Mangan's verse only adds to his ambiguous (if not shadowy) character. Precious little is truly known about the poet. He shunned companionship and few were close enough to have known him. Even his autobiographical fragments contain incongruities and anachronisms, enough to discredit their face value. Biographers have tended to describe a life based on Mangan's last ten most public years as ones gripped by mental and financial destitution.

That Mangan was a Dubliner is not in question. Discounting Moore and Joyce, Mangan scholar Brendan Clifford writes that the poet "is the one true Dubliner in the major literature of the world," (Clifford 7). This is true not only in that his life was confined to the city: unlike other great Irish writers, Mangan has had almost no reception in English literature. It is because Mangan is so much a product of Dublin—and nothing else—that Mangan is both "virtually unknown to world literature" (7) and practically forgotten in his own country. Contending that Ireland is ever looking to English literature to decide what writers to keep in print, and that, moreover, those writers in the canon—even Yeats—are really writing English literature, Clifford holds that Mangan's slight survival is owing to his preservation "at the firesides" of the Irish people. Clifford's take is a bit acerbic, but is at least some explanation as to why this important Dublin poet has been on the outside of anthologies and academic treatment.

Mangan was born to a schoolteacher-turned-grocer at the site of his parents shop, no. 3 Fishamble Street. The house is gone. His mother's family, Catholics in the cattle trade, had done well for themselves, so when the Mangans inherited the store they

had a good, cheap supplier. The grocery business was so lucrative that Mangan's father turned to land speculation, especially
around the vicinity of Lower Camden Street, though after a
stint of gross spending on parties and balls and a succession of
bad deals, he squandered what fortune they had. Young James
had some schooling in the better days, at Mr. Courtney's in
Derby Lane and at Mr. Browne's academy, no. 14 Chancery
Lane, but at fifteen he was compelled to take a job as a
scrivener's apprentice. He seems to have acquired his vast
knowledge of literature and languages later, under the auspices
of priests, and during his clerkship at the Trinity College library.

By his own account, he had a miserable childhood. He was
introverted and sickly, with paranoiac tendencies, "haunted by
an indescribable feeling of something terrible" (Mangan 9), that
only abetted his withdrawal from the society of others. His
family thought him mad, and if he had not yet reached that
state, Mangan records in his troubled autobiography that "the
seeds of that moral insanity were developed within me which
afterwards grew up into a tree of giant altitude" (15).

The extent to which Mangan's *Autobiography* is embellished
with the poet's creativity or insanity (written, probably, within a
year of his death) is not known. According to the text, his daily
life did not ameliorate his mental torture, but most scholars
hedge certain details: Mangan was, in his last years, in the
clutches of madness. He describes his apprenticeship to the
scrivener as a Dickensian hell. For three years he copied,
"[c]oerced to remain for the most part bound to one spot from
early morning till near midnight" (Mangan 19). These hours at
this time are unlikely, but the job of a scrivener for a person of
Mangan's creativity would have been a torment. In his family's
diminished circumstances, they moved into what Mangan
describes as "one of the dismallest domiciles perhaps to be met
with in the most forlorn recesses of any city in Europe," a leaky,
drafty, spider-infested hovel with dirt floors (19). His most fantastic account holds that, taken ill, he was forced to share a bed
with a leper. Real or not, Mangan attributes his lifelong

hypochondriasis to the episode and his subsequent contraction of some sort of skin disease.

Were things really that bad? He found time, somehow, to learn to write well. By the second half of the 1820s he began writing rhyming riddles in the "puzzler" periodicals of Dublin, and in the early 1830s he started contributing to the *Dublin Penny Journal*, a short-lived scholarly magazine of Irish antiquities. Its joint editors were George Petrie and John O'Donovan, with whom Mangan became friends. When Petrie came to head Dublin's Ordnance Survey he employed Mangan as a scribe, a position that offered the poet plenty of time in libraries, working closely with the literature of Ireland's past.

Petrie and his staff at the Ordnance Survey are among the most important scholars in this crucial period of ancient Irish historiography. Slated to document sites of historic interest, Petrie sent his team on archeological expeditions in the field and literary excursions in Dublin's libraries. O'Donovan did most of the field work; his brother-in-law Eugene O'Curry transcribed lore from ancient manuscripts; and Petrie, an illustrator among his other talents, drew ancient monuments and published papers about them. In the Ordnance Survey's short life, they collected over 400 volumes of material from ancient manuscripts, detailing Irish culture, language, and lore. Through Petrie's offices, a picture of ancient Ireland was formed, one drawn with the diligence of scientific inquiry. "[H]e is more important in the long run than Thomas Davis, Douglas Hyde, and perhaps even Yeats," notes Vivian Mercier in *Modern Irish Literature*. "The educated Irishman of the 1880s inherited a perception of his country's past that was influenced at every turn by Petrie ..." (Mercier 13–14).

Petrie's staff, especially O'Curry, supplied Mangan with prose translations of ancient Irish verse, and, having already displayed some skill in translation with his collection of German poems, he set out to transcribe the works of ancient bards into English. It is not known whether Mangan himself knew Gaelic. To confuse the matter further, he frequently relied on several English translations in composition. His "Dark Rosaleen," perhaps the most memorable of all his lyrics, drew heavily on Sir Samuel Ferguson's scholarship. Published in the *Nation* in 1846, the original was from a poet in the service of Hugh the Red O'Donnell, that Irish hero of Elizabethan times, in which the earl speaks to Ireland (Rosaleen) of his struggles for her.

The *Nation*, and later the *United Irishman*, printed some of Mangan's most nationalist poetry. "Siberia," for instance, likens famine-gripped Ireland to a wind-swept wasteland, with people too dead and frozen to "curse the Czar." And "To the Ingleezee Khafir, calling himself Djaun Bool Djenkinsun" is a jab at Great Britain disguised as a Persian translation: "Djaun Bool" is John Bull, a personification of England like America's Uncle Sam, and "Ingleezee Khafir" is the "English infidel," a term applied to British colonists in the Middle East.

The cholera epidemic of 1849 claimed Mangan's weak, troubled body. In his last years he was a skeleton walking Dublin's streets, pale, achy, with white hair under the huge black witch's hat he wore. The extent of his opium addiction is uncertain, but he surely drank a great deal, and there are stories of a few rousing nights shared with William Carleton on Wexford Street. Though there are conflicting accounts, he appears to have lived much of his short adult life in York Street, at no. 6. At some point he moved to despicable lodgings in Bride Street, from whence he was pried by a good old friend, Father Meehan, to die in a charity hospital at the age of forty-six. He is buried in Glasnevin Cemetery. A plaque marks his birthplace, and he is remembered by a bust by Oliver Sheppard in St. Stephen's Green.

Only a fraction of Mangan's more than 800 poems have survived to our day, and particularly troubling is the uneven nature of the poetry we do have. It is difficult from the body of work to discern his specific spiritual beliefs, and though he wrote much for the *Nation*, he was in fact a frequent contributor to the Tory *Dublin University Magazine*, for which he only stopped writing when his intemperance became too great a burden for either him or his editors. The magazine was founded in 1831 by Samuel Ferguson, among others, to promote conservative, Protestant views.

SAMUEL FERGUSON

The *DUM* was a vehicle for Ferguson's odd mixture of Irish antiquarianism and Anglo-Irish values, and, as such, Ferguson's commitment to the study of Irish literature requires some explaining. He was born in Belfast, 1810, strictly on the side of the Ascendancy, and came to Dublin to study law at Trinity College. For roughly the first thirty-five years of his life, he was devoted to preserving some vestige of Protestant rule in Ireland. O'Connell had just won Catholic Emancipation, and with his movement still sweeping through the country, it looked like the way of life Ferguson's family enjoyed—and for which many of his ancestors fought and died, protecting the interests of the Crown from the Popish mob—was quickly waning. Chief among vituperations from the newly empowered Catholics against Ferguson's class was the idea that the Ascendancy was comprised of interlopers, of aliens in Ireland. It was Ferguson's conviction that this was not the case. His family had been in Ireland for more than two hundred years; can they not be considered Irish? And are not the Celts immigrants to Ireland themselves? The trick for Ferguson was to establish the Irishness of the Anglo-Irish, and in this he advocated the study of Irish antiquities.

No great literature ever came from Ferguson's pen, though not for lack of trying. He did manage a few literal translations of Gaelic verse, with help from his friends Petrie and O'Curry, which he published in the *DUM*. "The Fairy Thorn" is likely considered the best of these early endeavors. In 1838 he published an anti-Catholic satire in *Blackwood's Edinburgh Magazine*, but that same year he was admitted to the bar, and subsequently found it difficult to continue writing. After seven years of silence he published "The Vengence of the Welshmen of Tiraway," and it was around this time that Ferguson reconsidered his unionist stance. Between the depredation of British policy during the potato famine and his first-hand experience of the mistreatment of Catholics in Dublin's courtrooms, Ferguson now sided with Irish nationalists. Many consider his belated 1847 elegy on the death of Thomas Davis to be his finest work.

Ferguson, eventually, had misgivings towards the violent means taken up by nationalist groups in the later nineteenth century. His "At the Polo-Ground," a poem published in 1882, was written to decry the gruesome assassinations of the newly appointed Chief Secretary for Ireland Lord Cavendish and his Under-Secretary Burke in Phoenix Park in May of that year. Still, the second half of his life was devoted to the collection of Irish folklore and the translation of ancient legends. After he married Mary Catherine Guinness in 1848, their home at 20 North Great George's Street became the nexus of Dublin's literary and intellectual life. He quit law altogether in 1867, was knighted for his work in antiquities in 1878, and made president of the Royal Irish Academy in 1882. Yeats was already publishing his first poems by the time Ferguson died, in 1886.

OSCAR WILDE

Though born in Dublin and educated at Trinity College, Wilde is perhaps best known for his obscenity trial in London, and indeed Wilde spent his most productive years in England. Born Oscar O'Flahertie Fingal Wills Wilde on October 16, 1854, in Dublin, Ireland, he was the younger son of Sir William and Lady Jane Wilde. His mother, a passionate and shrewd woman who evidently made a great impression upon her second son, was a poet herself, writing under the pseudonym *Speranza*. Lady Wilde held strong aesthetic and political beliefs, and she may very well have served as Wilde's earliest model for his female leads. His father, while renowned as a surgeon, was less credible in his domestic affairs and during Oscar's childhood, the Wilde family became the center of a sensational scandal when a former patient raised a charge of rape against Sir William.

In 1871, Wilde enrolled at Trinity College in Dublin where he excelled, placing first in his examinations in 1872. In 1874 Wilde won the Berkeley Gold Medal for Greek and was awarded a Demyship scholarship to Magdalen College in Oxford. The years from 1874–1878 were spent at Magdalen College, Oxford, where he received First Class degree in Classics and the Newdigate Prize for poetry with his submission of *Ravenna*. In London, the young Wilde cheerfully adopted an extravagant and flamboyant lifestyle, at times hailing a cab just to cross the street (the budding dramatist created spectacle as he breathed). Accordingly, Wilde's wardrobe was often central to his constant self-presentation. His clothes were ordered not from a tailor, but from theatre costumiers, and his often outlandish buttonholes of lilies, sunflowers, and green carnations—the underground symbol of aestheticism and homosexuality—became something of a trademark for this outrageous public persona. Yet despite his certain presence in London society, neither Wilde's first play, *Vera, or the Nihilists*, or his first volume of poetry was particularly well-received. Perhaps as a result of such professional disappointments, Wilde shifted into a more respectable Victorian lifestyle after the early 1880s.

In 1879, following the death of her husband, Lady Wilde moved to London where she became a part of a circle of Irish writers that included Shaw and Yeats. A talented linguist, poet, and Irish patriot, who had written several books and translated others, Lady Wilde's nom de plume was Speranza ('hope' in Italian) which came from her advocacy of the cause of Irish freedom. During her time in London she contributed articles and poems to *The Women's World*, a culture magazine for independent women.

During the 1880s, Oscar Wilde married Constance Lloyd, the daughter of a wealthy Irish barrister in 1884 and had two sons, Cyril and Vyvyan, in the following two years. Through the end of the decade, Wilde edited the fashion journal, *Women's*

World, and began publishing criticism and fiction—short stories and fairy tales that he wrote for his sons—in periodical press. In May, 1888, he published *The Happy Prince and Other Tales,* followed by "The Portrait of Mr. W.H." in 1889, and *The Picture of Dorian Gray,* his only novel, in 1890. Yet despite his outward presentation of social and domestic respectability, Oscar maintained a barely covert lifestyle of the brazen dandy. It was during these years that Robert Ross, who eventually published the first collected works of Oscar Wilde after the dramatist's death, was said to have introduced him to the practice of homosexuality.

As many critics and biographers have remarked, Oscar Wilde enjoyed being paradoxical. It is fitting, therefore, that the years recorded as perhaps his most flamboyant and reckless are also recognized as his period of greatest creative productivity. After *The Picture of Dorian Gray,* which received massive critical attention, Wilde went on to write *Salomé* and *Lady Windermere's Fan* in the following year, *A Woman of No Importance* in 1893, and *An Ideal Husband* and *The Importance of Being Earnest,* his dramatic masterpiece, in 1895. *Lady Windermere's Fan, A Woman of No Importance, An Ideal Husband,* and *The Importance of Being Earnest,* referred to collectively as Wilde's social comedies, simultaneously satirized contemporary social mores while sustaining them in apparent high regard. As a dramatist and a member of a notoriously artificial Society, Wilde relished the aspect of performance that imbibed the conventions of the day. At the opening night of *Lady Windermere's Fan,* Wilde confused and shocked his audience by making his curtain speech with a cigarette in hand; with his signature green-carnation buttonhole, he complimented them on the success of their performance, implying outrageously that the farce onstage extended to the seated audience.

Critics, often hung between admiration and outrage, were appropriately befuddled by this enigmatic persona, but Wilde seemed ultimately validated when several influential critics of the time, led by William Archer and A.B. Walkley, poured unambiguous praise upon his latest works. Still, Wilde did not enjoy his success for long. By the peak of his production in 1895 with *The Importance of Being Earnest*, Wilde faced a charge of sodomy raised by the Marquess of Queensbury, the father of a young man with whom the dramatist was passionately in love. After months of Wilde ignoring his warnings to stay away from his son, the infuriated Queensbury made public this aspect of Wilde's personal life that became his ruin. Wilde, strongly advised by his mother to defend himself, charged the Marquess with libel, but the evidence found against him proved absolutely damning, and after two trials—the first ending with a hung jury, and the second with a guilty verdict—Wilde was sentenced to two years of imprisonment and hard labor for his crime of "gross indecency," his affair with the young Lord Alfred Douglas.

During and after his imprisonment, from 1895–1897, Wilde himself concluded that he would never again be the same man who had produced the brilliance of the four social comedies or, perhaps more importantly, who possessed the personal energy that had inspired them. In prison, he wrote an extensive letter of confession and admonition addressed to Douglas, which was posthumously published as *De Profundis* by Robert Ross in 1905. But even this emotional epistle could not nearly comfort Wilde's great and growing grief at the losses of his life. His beloved mother died of acute bronchitis on February 3, 1896, and while she expressed constant support of her son, whom she recognized as tragically misunderstood, Wilde never recovered from the anguish and shame at his mother's death. By 1897, his wife, Constance, made her final separation with Oscar, and he was subsequently refused access to his sons, even after their mother's death in 1898.

After his release from prison, Wilde believed himself unfit for the society in which he had once thrived, and exiled himself to France, where he adopted the pseudonym "Sebastian Melmoth." Under this name, he published two letters in *The Daily Chronicle*, appealing to the public about cruelty to children in British prisons. His final work is a return to poetry, entitled *The*

Ballad of Reading Gaol, which he intended to produce for himself a "sacramental" value of intimacy and reconciliation following his experience of imprisonment as a criminal. *The Ballad of Reading Gaol* was a popular success and may have quickened the personal redemption that the dramatist-poet desired. After a trip to Rome in 1900, Wilde fell suddenly and feverishly ill. He died on November 30, 1900, after a deathbed baptism into the Roman Catholic Church in his Paris hotel.

In light of the apparent frivolity of his most famous works, the social comedies, and the sensationalism of his trials, it may often be forgotten that Oscar Wilde, in addition to his writings as a poet and dramatist, also wrote important works of criticism. "The Decay of Lying" (1889) and "The Critic as Artist" (1890) are his best-known essays, collected in the 1891 volume entitled *Intentions*. The four essays in this volume examine art and criticism from a theoretical or philosophical, rather than strictly practical, perspective, and conclude that the spheres of art and ethics are, or should be, entirely distinct and separate. Championing art's autonomy, Oscar Wilde consciously, if not entirely overtly, turned nineteenth-century English aesthetic and social convention on its head with a skillful combination of outrage and subtlety that brought his audience into his dramatic addresses, often without their noticing their crucial role in the play.

CHAPTER SIX

Yeats and the Irish
Literary Revival

Whether it is called the Irish literary revival, or the Celtic Revival, or the Celtic Renaissance, or sometimes a combination of the above, a literary movement began in Dublin in the late nineteenth century that produced some of the greatest and most important works in the English language. The idea, generally speaking, was to look to the Gaelic past, to legend and literature, and to the folklore and traditions of the Irish peasantry for the inspiration to create a new Irish literature. The Revival owes much to the works of Ferguson and Petrie, and Mangan and the later Standish James O'Grady, and others working in the translation of Irish poetry, but it is a mistake to posit a direct line between the poets and writers of the mid-nineteenth century and the authors who took the themes and content of the older Gaelic literature to the rest of the English-speaking world. Yeats, for instance, treats Mangan as his "discovery." It is not that the Dublin writers of a generation earlier were so forgettable; rather, these former writers were cloistered and practically unknown to English literature. The individuals of the literary revival, those who took Irish culture to English literature, were mostly of Anglo-Irish, Protestant backgrounds, a new audience for the earlier literary archeologists, but one with the tools to establish a tradition of Irish culture within English literature.

Yeats and Synge, and Æ, Lady Gregory, Douglas Hyde, James Stephens (not the earlier patriot but the novelist and poet), George Moore, and later Sean O'Casey and James Joyce, all swept Dublin with their work. Almost everybody wrote either within the scope of the Revival or in response to it. The movement controlled the cultural machinery of the city for more than forty years, and perhaps it was the nature of its intellectual community that made Dublin more susceptible to a preoccupation with a singular movement than other cities. In *Scholars and Rebels of Nineteenth Century Ireland*, Terry Eagleton wrote of the peculiar intimacy of Dublin's intelligentsia, a group with similar interests and backgrounds that met and talked in ad hoc clubs and in each other's dining rooms. The thinking people of Dublin were much like a small town, and their town hall was Leinster House on Kildare Street. Built for the Duke of Leinster in 1745, in an ironically appropriate politics-to-culture move, it was sold to the Royal Dublin Society after the Act of Union, becoming the cultural omphalos of the city for the next hundred years. Buildings dedicated to the arts and sciences sprang up all around Leinster House, cultural institutions dominated by a cabal of familiar people. Eagleton describes its influence in terms of a sort of personality cult, revered by the rest of the city. "A few close-knit individuals could thus define an entire culture" (Eagleton 43). And that is just what Yeats and his coterie set out to do.

WILLIAM BUTLER YEATS

W.B. Yeats's twentieth year was to dictate the course of his life and the future of Irish literature. At the time he was studying to be a painter at the Metropolitan School of Art, Kildare Street, where his father, John B. Yeats, a struggling painter himself, had taken a teaching job. Though he had been born in Dublin at 5 Sandymount Avenue (the three-storey still stands), his father's search for work as a painter and his family's frequent vacations in Sligo meant that most of his formative years were spent between metropolitan London and Sligo's Irish countryside, with its faeries and folktales. Financial difficulties had forced John B. Yeats back to the less expensive Dublin in 1881; he opened a studio at 44 York Street, and Willie (as he was then called) went to Erasmus Smith High School, Harcourt Street. Having earned some reputation as a painter, the elder Yeats frequented Dublin's intellectual circles, often taking his son along. In 1885, W.B. accompanied John B. to a meeting of the Contemporary Club, where the younger Yeats first met the old Fenian named John O'Leary.

O'Leary enchanted Yeats. He was wise, gruff, intellectual, and had endured prison and exile for his country. Convicted of publishing treasonable documents, O'Leary opted for a shorter prison sentence (five years) on the condition that he leave his beloved Ireland. He had just returned to Dublin from a fifteen-year Parisian exile earlier in 1885, and he had a thing or two to say about nationalism and literature.

The Fenians took their name from *Fiann*, the ancient Irish army of legend. It was founded first in America in 1858 by Irish émigrés and gainied a Dublin chapter later that same year. Funded by Irish-American money and supported by the starving rural populace, the Fenians all but gave up on legislative measures, resorting to militancy to achieve a free Ireland. John O'Leary, along with Charles Kickham, James Stephens, and Jeremiah O'Donovan Rossa, were arrested for treason in 1865 for publishing the Fenian newspaper *The Irish People*. A Fenian-sponsored rising in 1867 was quickly quelled, but it won the attention of the prime minister, William Gladstone, who made concessions to improve the miserable predicament of Irish tenants with the first Irish Land Act; the disestablishment of the Church of Ireland as the state church soon followed. By the time O'Leary returned to Dublin, the Fenians and other nationalist groups had thrown their support to the political wizardry of Charles Stewart Parnell, whose maneuvering for the Irish cause held more promise than anything the Fenians had done in the 1860s.

According to Yeats, O'Leary took to the nationalist movement not because he believed their actions would bring about an Irish republic, but because he thought the cause of nationalism, its ability to strengthen the spirit, was good for the moral character of the Irish people. At issue, first and last for O'Leary, was the dignity of the individual. Hence O'Leary's maxim— Yeats enjoyed evincing such pithy sincerities from the old man—that Yeats would take up as the rule for his artistic life:

> Once when I was defending an Irish politician who had made a great public outcry because he was treated as a common felon he said, "There are things that a man must not do to save a nation." He would speak a sentence like that in ignorance of its passionate value, and would forget it the moment after. (Yeats, *Autobiographies* 3:101)

It was an admonition against the compromise of one's art, and by extension one's self, for the sake of a cause. If the benefit of fighting for nationhood is the betterment of moral character, then writing bad poetry—an assault on dignity itself—is self-defeating. It is something one must not do. Yeats elaborated in his later autobiography, *The Trembling of the Veil* (1922), writing that, "... he no more wished to strengthen Irish Nationalism by second-rate literature than by second-rate morality.... [W]hen I asked what things, he said, 'To cry in public,' and I think it probable that he would have added, if pressed, 'To write oratorical or insincere verse,'" (*Autobiographies* 3:178). O'Leary introduced the history of Ireland into Yeats's work, charmed him with the possibility of building a culture from the old traditions, but warned the young man to keep nationalism at arm's length from his poetry.

Yeats had just begun to publish a few poems in the *Dublin University Review* when he met O'Leary, but he was still studying to be a painter. O'Leary's sponsorship saw more of Yeats's poetry into that publication. Moreover, the twenty-year-old had not heard of Thomas Davis or his poetry until O'Leary lent him a volume of the poetry of the Young Irelanders, and while "he did not ... claim that they were very good" (*Autobiographies* 3:100), O'Leary presented Davis as a well-meaning patriot. Yet the work Ferguson, Davis, Standish James O'Grady, and others had done in Gaelic literature appealed to the sentiment for Irish folklore Yeats had developed in Sligo. Given the family's financial predicament, the modest money Yeats could earn by writing and anthologizing made O'Leary's nudge all that was necessary to move Yeats into literature.

One of Yeats's friends at the Metropolitan School of Art, George Russell—better known by his pseudonym Æ—was also interested in poetry, and was in fact a real Dublin renaissance man when he entered public life. A painter, poet, journalist, essayist, and economist, Russell with Yeats shared an interest in the occult, a surprising but important influence on the writers of the Revival in a country with such deep-seated opinions on religious matters. Æ had early on shucked Christianity because he believed God's punishment unjust, and in his later teens he began to have visions he associated with the ancient gods of Ireland, which led him deeper into theosophical study. (The chance origin of Æ's pseudonym is rooted in his esoteric sensibilities: the story goes that he heard the word *Æon* whispered as he was mesmerized by one of his own paintings; later at the National Library he found a dictionary opened to the right page, and read that its Gnostic sense referred to the first beings created in the universe. He signed a letter to the periodical *Lucifer* in 1888 with the pseudonym, confusing the proofreader who queried "AE—?," and the diphthong stuck.) Even though Yeats and Æ were often on opposing sides of the literary movement they helped to create, their own highly developed spiritualism, rooted in esotericism and reverence for nature, would be the single most important influence on their poetry. They founded the Dublin Hermetic Society jointly in that fateful year, 1885. Their friend Charles Johnston, the Dublin mystic, established the Dublin Lodge of the Theosophical Society the next year, and both became members.

YEATS AND Æ

Partly a reaction to the seeming sovereignty of science in the late nineteenth century, partly to J.S. Mill's philosophy, and partly to the iconoclasm of Darwin's theories of evolution, theosophy—with all its alleged connections to an uncorrupted pagan past—was easily reconciled with the study of Irish folklore and the production of poetry. Yeats, who was particularly troubled by his father's positivism, saw the connections between old literature, new literature, and esoterism immediately. He later wrote, "I had, when we first made our Society, proposed for our consideration that whatever the great poets had affirmed in their finest moments was the nearest we could come to an authoritative religion, and that their mythology, their spirits of water and wind, were but literal truth," (*Autobiographies* 3:97). Good literature, which was, of course, Yeats's intent, was nothing short of truth. Their fathers were not amused; each thought his son's friend lured the other into what was at best an absurdity. In fact it was John Yeats's old college friend, Edward Dowden, a frequent visitor to his York Street studio, who led Yeats and Æ into theosophy. Professor Dowden's late biography of Shelley and the account of his dabbling in the occult at Eton College first inspired the young poets to try to conjure the spirits of Ireland's ancient hero-gods. Yeats and Æ later visited Dowden at his home, where the professor introduced them to *Esoteric Buddhism*, written by the Blavatskian A.P. Sinnett. The two later distanced themselves from that great charlatan, Madame Helena Petrova Blavatsky and her brand of theosophy—Æ was the first to back off—but Sinnett's book remained an important early influence.

Yeats was in fact on a maddened quest for concrete evidence of the otherworldly, seeking more contact with the supernatural that Blavatsky sanctioned. At one Dublin séance early in 1888 Yeats suffered a horrible trauma, becoming so terrified that he tried to say a prayer, but, able to remember none, he could only recite the opening lines of *Paradise Lost* to see him through. From his letters it is clear that the experience was mentally scarring, though he still sought out esoteric truth, leaving behind the chicanery of Madame Blavatsky. He was active with the Theosophists long enough to inject an Indian flavor in his early collection, *Crossways*.

Yeats dashed between London and Dublin until 1896, when he came to stay with Lady Augusta Gregory in her home at Coole Park. Russell, meanwhile, left art school to take a job as a draper's assistant at Pim Brothers, South Great George's Street. A month before Blavatsky died, Æ moved into 8 Ely Place, known as Ely House or the Household, a home owned by Annie and Frederick Dicks that served as the Dublin headquarters for the Theosophical Society. Russell lived here for most of the 1890s, leaving when he married another resident of the Household, Violet North. Today it is the meeting house for the Knights of St. Colambanus, a Catholic society, and at least some of the murals by Æ adorning its walls survive.

George Moore, another cultural giant of the time whose autobiographical *Hail and Farewell* is a wealth of information on the figures of the Irish Literary Revival, lived nearby at 4 Ely Place. The home once belonged to the famous lawyer John Philpot Curran, whose daughter embarrassed the venerable attorney with her scandalous relationship with the rebel Robert Emmet. George Moore caused all sorts of trouble in the cul-de-sac, as related by Yeats in *Dramatis Personae* (1935). He painted his front door green despite an agreement between landlords and householders that all the doors in the neighborhood be painted white. The action, which Moore defended on the grounds that he was an art critic, earned the ire of two sisters who shared a home nearby. They bought his novel, *Esther Waters*, tore it to bits, and shoved it in Moore's mailbox in an envelope that read "too filthy to keep in the house." In retaliation Moore got up thrice nightly to bang on the sisters' iron railings with a stick so their dog would bark. The sisters then hired an organ grinder to play under Moore's window while he wrote, after which Moore threatened legal measures against the organ grinder. Moore also owned the garden across the street where he often sat and held parties, and enjoyed the singing of a favorite blackbird. After a time Moore became worried that the sisters' cat might get his blackbird. He assailed the animal with stones, but when it proved elusive (Moore worried that the cat got up too early) he set a trap. Yeats ran into a despairing Moore later on: "'Remember that trap?' 'Yes.' 'Remember that bird?' 'Yes.' 'I have caught the bird'" (*Autobiographies* 3:328–329).

Both Yeats and Æ imagined a metaphysical change coming as the new century approached, with literature acting as a catalyst. Russell wrote to Yeats in 1896:

> You remember my writing to you about the awakening of the ancient fires which I knew about. Well, it has been confirmed from other sources and we are likely to publish it. The gods have returned to Erin and have centered themselves in the sacred mountains and blow the fires through the country. They have been seen by several in vision, they will awaken the magical instinct everywhere, and the universal heart of the people will turn to the old druidic beliefs.... Out of Ireland will arise a light to transform many ages and peoples.... I believe profoundly that a new Avatar is about to appear ..."
> (Russell 17)

And Yeats in 1898 predicted a "crowning crisis" for the world. In constrast to Darwinian evolution, Yeats believed that man had been devolving from a former age of revelation and truth, and that the trend was about to reverse; that the world was

> at the moment when man is about to ascend, with the wealth he has been so long gathering upon his shoulders, the stairway he has been descending from the first days....
>
> The arts are, I believe, about to take upon their shoulders the burdens that have fallen from the shoulders of priests, and to lead us back upon our journey by filling our thoughts with the essences of things, and not with things (Yeats, *Essays and Introductions* 192)

It is a privileged place for art and literature, but a still greater role for the literature of Ireland. Yeats thought that by reclaiming the ideas of the ancient Irish, ideas which survive in folklore and poetry, the Irish people would lead humanity back to its higher, truer existence. He proselytized, though, on a practical level, claiming that the ancient Celtic literature made for good, innovative writing. In his 1897 essay *The Celtic Element in Literature* he wrote:

> literature dwindles to a mere chronicle of circumstance, or passionless fantasies, and passionless meditations, unless it is constantly flooded with the passions and beliefs of ancient times, and that of all the fountains of the passions and beliefs of ancient times in Europe, the Slavonic, the Finnish, the Scandinavian, and the Celtic, the Celtic alone has been for centuries close to the main river of European literature. (*Essays and Introductions* 185)

This was the entry point for a sort of historical nationalism in Yeats's spiritual and artistic systems, and it helped to marry nationalist ideas into the Literary Revival.

While he endorsed a messianic role for the Irish people through a renewed culture, Yeats was wary of venturing into political nationalism, though he would be impelled to do so by the most beautiful woman in Ireland. His love for the revolutionary Maud Gonne inspired his most political plays and poems, though it was never enough for her. She rejected Yeats's marriage proposals at least three times. He turned to Gonne's illegitimate daughter Iseult, whom Gonne passed off as her niece, but Yeats was too fatherly to Iseult, and she likewise declined his proposal. Yeats loved Maud for the rest of his life.

While Yeats turned out his early verse, consisting mostly of earthy peregrinations into nature and Irish myth, he was also busy anthologizing and criticizing the Irish writers of the past. It was more work than anyone else had done to create a canon of Irish literature for academics, and it laid the foundations for his contemporaries to both subsume the Irish literary past and create a literature of their own Ireland. He had clout enough by 1894 to launch Æ as a poet. That the Revival is usually dated from 1885, the year of Yeats's first published poetry, to 1939, the year of his death, evidences his central role in the movement.

THE IRISH NATIONAL THEATRE

Lady Gregory, with whom Yeats was living after 1896, was a collector of folklore in her own right. The two had met in London in 1894 and remained friends for the rest of their lives. From an Ascendancy family, Gregory had been widowed since 1892, an event she admitted was necessary to give her the freedom to write. Working with Gregory, Yeats's poetry became less lofty. She had taken up the cause of Home Rule, and by 1898 Gregory, Yeats, and the Catholic dramatist Edward Martyn were discussing plans for an Irish National Theatre to further Irish cultural autonomy. Dublin had never developed a strong tradition in drama—certainly nothing beyond mimicry of the stages of London—and they saw the development of a theater germane to Ireland as an important contribution to Irish culture, a prerequisite to nationhood.

Given Yeats's early ideas of the reality of, say, Celtic hero-gods or the messianic future of Ireland, the practical application of literature in the struggle for statehood might seem doubtful. But while these grand notions led Yeats to consider the importance of Irishness, the selling-point of the new literary movement was the establishment of an independent Irish culture. Æ, who was vice-president of the Irish National Theatre for a time, distilled this idea in one of his editorials, writing that "A nation exists primarily because of its own imagination of itself," (quoted in Kain, 26). At the turn of the nineteenth century political movements toward Home Rule had gone stagnant, and the culture-building undertaken by the figures of the Irish literary revival appealed to nationalists as a way to validate an Irish nation.

Renting Dublin's Ancient Concert Rooms on Pearse Street in 1899, the Irish National Theatre staged its first plays, Yeats's *The Countess Cathleen* and Martyn's *The Heather Field.* In what would become a trend for the theater, controversy erupted immediately. In *The Countess Cathleen,* Irish peasants enduring a famine sell their souls to demons in exchange for food. The idea that the peasantry would betray their faith in adversity offended several groups, including Dublin's Catholic potentates. Demonstrations were held outside the theatre on opening night, but in the end the play was a success.

But the practical aspects of running an avant-garde stage in Dublin caught up with the Irish National Theatre after three seasons. In 1901 audiences were disappointed with the lack of Irish acting talent (most actors were local amateurs). It was George Russell and Maud Gonne who saved the theatre from certain collapse. At the request of Frank and William Fay, whose Irish National Dramatic Company had been finding and training Irish actors for the Irish stage for years in their small productions, Æ wrote two scenes for their play *Deirdre.* Russell introduced the Fay brothers to Yeats and Gregory, and they set *Deirdre* on a double-bill with Yeats's *Cathleen ni Houlihan,* a nationalist drama. Both plays were supported by a cast from Maud Gonne's radical nationalist group, *Inghinidhe na hEireann,* the Daughters of Ireland. Russell did the backdrops and the costumes, Gonne took the lead role as Yeats's Cathleen, and Maire Quinn played the Irish heroine Deirdre. The success of these shows produced in early April, 1902, at St. Teresa's Hall on Clarendon Street, ensured the existence of the rechristened Irish National Theatre Company for years to come. Taking over the Mechanic's Institute on Abbey Street in 1903, the Company gained a new, permanent home, and took the name by which it is known today, the Abbey Theatre. A fire in 1951 gutted the backstage during a performance of Sean O'Casey's *The Plough and the Stars,* but after fifteen years a government grant was secured for the Abbey's new home. Inside today visitors can see portraits of many of the figures connected with the Abbey's success.

Yeats's Nobel Banquet Speech

I have been all my working life indebted to the Scandinavian nation. When I was a very young man, I spent several years writing in collaboration with a friend the first interpretation of the philosophy of the English poet Blake. Blake was first a disciple of your great Swedenborg and then in violent revolt and then half in revolt, half in discipleship. My friend and I were constantly driven to Swedenborg for an interpretation of some obscure passage, for Blake is always in his mystical writings extravagant, paradoxical, obscure. Yet he has had upon the last forty years of English imaginative thought the influence which Coleridge had upon the preceding forty; and he is always in his poetry, often in his theories of painting, the interpreter or the antagonist of Swedenborg. Of recent years I have gone to Swedenborg for his own sake, and when I received your invitation to Stockholm, it was to his biography that I went for information. Nor do I think that our Irish theatre could have ever come into existence but for the theatre of Ibsen and Bjørnson. And now you have conferred upon me this great honour. Thirty years ago a number of Irish writers met together in societies and began a remorseless criticism of the literature of their country. It was their dream that by freeing it from provincialism they might win for it European recognition. I owe much to those men, still more to those who joined our movement a few years later, and when I return to Ireland these men and women, now growing old like myself, will see in this great honour a fulfilment of that dream. I in my heart know how little I might have deserved it if they had never existed.

http://nobelprize.org/literature/laureates/1923/
yeats-speech.html

JOHN MILLINGTON SYNGE

Yeats won the Nobel Prize for Literature in 1923, and though it was awarded for all his work, it is clear in his Nobel Lecture that he considered the influence of his National Theatre far more important in the history of Ireland than any of his verse. But in his speech he is quick to credit the success of the Theatre to many patrons, players, and playwrights, none more than that "strange man of genius" Yeats had met in Paris, John Millington Synge. Synge, whose plays set the Irish stage ablaze, was studying French literature at the Sorbonne when he met Yeats, who convinced the young playwright to look to the rural poor of his own country for inspiration. He spent several summers in the Aran Islands, learning the dialect and character of the inhabitants that later had so much to do with the success of his plays. *In the Shadow of the Glen*, the first of Synge's peasant plays to be performed, was the story of an old farmer and his adulterous young wife. Controversy shrouded its first staging at the Abbey Theatre, with the future first president of the Irish Free State, Arthur Griffith, among the most vociferous critics, calling it "a slur on Irish womanhood." But conservative backlash against Synge's first play was paltry compared to the week-long rioting that ensued during performances of *The Playboy of the Western World* in 1907. In it, the protagonist Christy kills his father with a spade in a fit of passion. He flees to a Mayo village, where he is lionized for his crime. Along with a risqué line that imagined Irish women in their underwear, the idea that Irish peasants would so readily welcome a murderer, and a parricidal one at that, caused endemic overreaction. It took an on-stage lecture from Yeats to quell the crowds.

Synge was born outside the city in Rathfarnham, moving a little closer to Dublin when Synge was still a boy, to 4 Orwell Park—the same home once inhabited by a young Bram Stoker. He attended Mr. Herrick's school in Dublin for a time, but with a weak constitution his formative education was irregular, and he was tutored mostly at home. Despite consigning himself to music, Synge studied Irish and Hebrew at Trinity College. At

Coblenz in 1893 he reconsidered, and decided to pursue literature. He met Yeats in Paris in 1896 but had his first attack of
Hodgkin's disease, a kind of cancer, the following year, which
made his trips to the hard-lived Aran Islands even more difficult. More or less confined to Dublin in his last years, Synge
succumbed to Hodgkin's at Elpis Hospital in the spring of
1909, just shy of his thirty-eighth birthday.

Æ AND JAMES STEPHENS

Deirdre was Æ's only foray in to drama. In 1897, Sir Horace
Plunkett, a Dublin legislator, enlisted his help in the Irish Agricultural Organization Society, where Æ worked as an economist
establishing agricultural cooperatives, especially among the
peasants of western Ireland. In 1905 he became editor of the
Society's journal, the *Irish Homestead,* a weekly publication as
eclectic as its editor, where Æ discussed opinions on politics,
published new farming techniques, and launched new Irish
writers. The *Homestead* was Russell's primary concern for nearly
twenty years, but he remained active in literary and theosophist
circles.

Most of his earlier poetry has always had a limited audience,
with references to Hindu gods and homages to theosophical
divinities that meant a lot to initiates, but sounded vague and
redundant to many modern readers. *The Divine Vision and
Other Poems* (1904), his third collection, finds inspiration in
natural surroundings, but also reveals his exposure to the people
and folklore of western Ireland's countryside. The year 1913 saw
the successful publication of *Collected Poems,* which included
several new poems set in Dublin. Four years later he finished
The Candle of Vision, a prose account of his mystical experiences
that is far more effective than any of his attempts in verse. Æ's
poetry improved as he grew older, but the prose of *The Candle*
and his articles for the *Homestead* and his later, broader weekly,
the *Irish Statesman,* are superior.

Thus, Russell is remembered more as a Dublin figurehead, a cul-
tivator of the literature of the Revival rather than as a contributor

to that literature. His penchant for discovering and fostering new young writers became a sort of joke around Dublin after a while. "The greatest pleasure I find in life is discovering new young poets," he wrote in 1908 to Kathryn Tynan, who was close to many of the writers of the Celtic Renaissance (Russell 65–66). He was the first to give James Joyce a chance. One story has it that in August 1902, it was nearly midnight when someone knocked at his door at 25 Coulson Avenue, Rathgar, where he and Violet moved after they were married. The young man at the door introduced himself as James Joyce, and asked Æ if it was too late to come in for a chat, to which Æ replied that it was never too late. Joyce shared his poems and stories, and the men talked past four in the morning (with lots of Yeats-bashing from Joyce, allegedly). Æ invited Joyce to write stories for his *Irish Homestead*, a few of which wound up in *Dubliners*. Joyce cutely remembered his debt to Æ in *Ulysses* with the pun, "A.E.I.O.U."

By 1908, Russell was looking around Dublin for another protégé, an answer to Yeats's Synge in their not-so-friendly rivalry. Arthur Griffith, founder of the Sinn Fein party and later the first president of the Irish Free State, had been printing a weekly called the *United Irishman*, and Æ vowed to find his newest talent within its pages. He did. That year he walked into the Dublin offices of the Mecredy law firm, and told the tiny clerk behind the typewriter that he wished to see Mr. Stephens, to which the clerk replied, "I am he." Russell wrote to Tynan excitedly:

> I have discovered a new young poet in a fellow called James Stephens who has a real original note in him. He has had the devil of a time poor fellow. Works about fourteen hours a day for twenty shillings and is glad to get it. Was out of work for a year once and went homeless and hungry and was saved from starving by a woman who sold fruit from a stall. Good education for the soul but sometimes bad for the body. (Russell 65)

Æ would always be Stephens's mentor. He paraded the short, young, courteous poet around Dublin, where Stephens impressed literary circles with his charm and left everyone wondering where he had amassed such considerable learning. Stephens told everybody that he was born on February 2, 1882—that he shared a birthday with James Joyce—but he was probably born sometime in 1880, and he probably knew it too. Stephens was always reticent and often enigmatic about his origins: it was his conviction that art should be approached with objectivity, and that the life and personality of the writer are insignificant to the work. Careful biographers have revealed that he was probably born near St. Catherine's Church, at 5 Thomas Court, where his parents were living in 1880. He never knew his father, who died of phthisis when Stephens was two. After this he suffered the neglect of his mother, who probably framed him for begging in the street, a crime which had him taken away to the Meath Protestant Industrial School for Boys when he was six years old. He never saw his mother again. Getting into such a school was considered (by just about everybody) to be a lucky thing, since there boys were offered an education and preparation for work in the trades. Stephens spent ten years at Meath, just outside Dublin, where he made some friends, enjoyed the school's meager library, and began a lifelong interest in gymnastics. When he left in the spring of 1896 he went to live with two brothers—friends from school—with their mother on York Street.

York Street then was a tenement row, with a good side and a worse side, and the Collins family lived at the better end, not far from John Yeats's studio. Stephens took a job as a junior clerk for a lawyer, Mr. Wallace, at 9 Eustace Street, the first of many clerkships he held all over Dublin. But, a natural storyteller, Stephens longed to write. He read everything he could get his hands on. He saved candy wrappers and asked at grocers for white paper for scribbling stories and poems.

By 1901 he came to think that if he were ever to become a good writer he should be detached and even uncomfortable, so he left York Street and his friends. This begins a period of biographical obscurity, one encouraged by Stephens, who often told whimsical stories about himself to the inquiring literary community. He was once so hungry that he fought with a dog for a loaf of bread. He would hide beyond the gates of St. Stephens Green after dark with other Dublin indigents to try to catch ducks. In despair after frequent rejections from publishers, he threw himself into the Liffey one night, changed his mind while in the water and barely made it to shore, where he was saved by the graces of a prostitute, who gave him food and a bed. It is difficult to say how much of this is true. The only paper trail Stephens left is, appropriately, a library lending register that lists a change of residence after 1901 to an address on Portobello Road.

Arthur Griffith finally published Stephens in 1905. He met the publisher a year or two later and must have made an impression, since his prose and poetry became regular contributions in both *The United Irishman* and Griffith's second periodical, *Sinn Fein*, which came up when authorities suppressed *The United Irishman* for content that made them nervous. Though Griffith's brand of nationalism was a peaceful one, in his paper he advised that elected Irish MPs set up a congress in Ireland, and legislate from there. It happened in 1919, and leaders created the office of president for their new polity in 1922, calling it the Irish Free State. Arthur Griffith became the first president of this hard-fought, long-awaited, quasi-national status, a precursor to the Republic of Ireland. That Griffith, a literary man, took the helm of the new government speaks volumes to the Irish regard for its literati, and is only one instance where politics and literature meet. Congreve held sinecures, and Richard Brinsley Sheridan viewed his seat in the House of Commons as another stage. In the twentieth century Æ did such impressive work in agriculture that he is remembered by a plaque on the Plunkett building; William Butler Yeats sat in the Irish Senate after 1922; and Douglas Hyde, the Celtic scholar, was the only plausible choice for President of the Republic of Ireland in 1937.

Over Hyde's long life (1860–1949) he did as much as anyone else to sway Irish culture. He was a regular fixture in the circles of the 1880s and 1890s that defined the place of Ireland in literature and the place of literature in Ireland. Though born to a Protestant minister in County Roscommon, Hyde learned the Irish language from local speakers, and, after excelling in Latin, Greek, and German at Trinity College, Hyde formed the Gaelic League in 1893 in the interest of reviving the Irish language. To this end, he made Gaelic required for entry into the National University of Ireland, and wrote plays and poems in Irish. The name *Sinn Fein*—meaning "ourselves alone"—is taken from the last verse of his poem "Waiting for Help," and his Irish-language play *An Tincéar and an tSigbeóg* ("The Tinker and the Fairy") was performed in George Moore's garden at Ely Place to jeers from the windows of Unionist neighbors (which, of course, delighted Moore). Hyde's *History of Irish Literature* (1899) anthologized only Gaelic writers, for he believed that if a new Irish culture should arise it would be rooted in the Irish language. (This was too big a pill for Yeats to swallow, who thought that reviving Gaelic on a national scale was impossible, and was apparently incapable himself of learning the language.) Despite his proximity to the Revival and its nationalist tones, though, Hyde did his best to shun politics. He served as president of his own Gaelic League until 1915, resigning because it had become, by then, little more than a political organization. In the turbulent opening decades of the twentieth century Hyde immersed himself in academics, though his spotless reputation only made him more attractive to Irish politics. He took a seat in the Senate of the Irish Free State, and when the office of the president was created for the Republic of Ireland in 1937, the venerable Hyde was the choice of all parties.

Stephens's first novel, *The Charwoman's Daughter*, was published serially in the *Irish Review* in 1911 as *Mary, Mary*, and was published as a book in 1912. *The Crock of Gold*, probably his best known prose work, followed in 1913, and *The*

Demi-Gods was published the next year. Once famous, Stephens went on lecture tours to America almost yearly, but whether he ever left Dublin before that is not known, and most of his prose until 1920 is set in Dublin. The best treatment of Stephens's attitudes toward the city is scholar Stephen Putzel's essay *James Stephens's Paradoxical Dublin*, which expounds the author's view of the city as at once repulsive for its squalor and poverty and beautiful for its function as a nexus of art and culture. *The Charwoman's Daughter*, which smacks of a fairy tale, has Mary Makebelieve moving from the sensual, Edenic gardens of Phoenix Park to the hungry Dublin slums. *Here are the Ladies*, Stephens's collection of short stories, has an undeniable affinity to James Joyce's *Dubliners*: the stories are of Dublin's middle class in a claustrophobic city, one they need to move from or beyond to grow in spirit. *The Crock of Gold*, superficially a mixed-up leprechaun story, has been explained by critics as an updated incarnation of Blakean mysticism. It too makes of Dublin a dim metropolis, full of materialistic and spiritless people. In the end the ancient gods of Ireland return to rescue the Philosopher from meaningless urbanity, calling for others to escape:

> Come to us, ye lovers of life and happiness. Hold out thy hand—a brother shall seize it from afar. Leave the plough and the cart for a little time: put aside the needle and the awl—is leather thy brother, O man? ... Come away! come away! from the loom and the desk, from the shop where the carcasses are hung, from the place where raiment is sold and the place where it is sewn in darkness: O bad treachery! Is it for joy you sit in the broker's den, thou pale man? Has the attorney enchanted thee? ... Come away! for the dance has begun lightly, the wind is sounding over the hill, the sun laughs down into the valley, and the sea leaps upon the shingle, panting for joy, dancing, dancing, dancing for joy....
> (Stephens, *The Crock of Gold* 227–228)

But there were far more pernicious forces than enchanting attorneys brewing in Dublin around 1915. Armed rebellion was in the air.

THE EASTER REBELLION

John Redmond, Parnell's successor and Ireland's leader in the British Parliament, had fought hard within the confines of the legislature for Home Rule. When in 1912 it appeared that Redmond would secure enough votes to pass a Home Rule bill, Sir Edward Carson declared the resistance of Ulster and raised a Unionist army, threatening civil war should any autonomous legislation include Ulster. Nationalists countered with their own army in Dublin, but the outbreak of World War I prevented the Home Rule Act from taking effect, side-stepping civil war. Redmond then made a miscalculation, one that, for Stephens, held him accountable for the insurrection that gripped Dublin for a week in 1916: he pledged the support of the Irish with the British in the Great War raging on the Continent. The majority of the Irish population was in fact ready to set aside their long-standing difference with Great Britain for the Great War, with tens of thousands of Irish joining English forces in France. But some nationalist factions had had enough of Redmond. Rumors of an imminent rising against the ruling English flitted about Dublin for years until it actually happened on April 24, 1916. James Stephens, with the attention of a journalist and the subtlety of a poet, set out to write a prose account of the city under siege. He had a bird's-eye view from his lodgings at 42 Fitzwilliam Place, and his *Insurrection in Dublin*, published the following year, gives a most compelling vision of the rising as experienced by Dubliners.

The insurrection took everyone by surprise. Police and government officials were caught off guard, many vacationing out of town for the long Easter weekend. After a quiet morning, Stephens lunched at home, and was on his way back to his office at the National Gallery (he had recently taken a job as its Registrar) when he discovered that the Volunteers had rushed and captured many buildings in Dublin. They built roadblocks, paralyzing transit in, out, and within the city.

Stephens's account demonstrates throughout the ignorance of Dublin denizens regarding any real details of the uprising. All news was hearsay. How many rebels held the city? There could be three dozen or three thousand men in St. Stephens Green. Rumor had it that the Volunteers had been successful all over Ireland; that they had complete control of Cork; that German submarines dotted Ireland's coastlines and troop ships had landed on the eastern seaboard to aid Ireland in a war with England. Some of these rumors were easily discounted (Stephens jokes that someone had spotted a German submarine in the pond in St. Stephen's Green), but around Dublin the tricolor flag of the Republic flew, police had vanished, and the British military had not yet shown up in any number.

Dubliners who dared to take a side were largely against the rebels for the most personal and pragmatic reasons: they had commandeered many cars, trucks, and other vehicles from civilians at gunpoint, and the blockades they built with these masses of metal made life in the city difficult. Food shortages started early on in the week. Moreover, the Volunteers were not beyond committing acts of violence against civilians to maintain control. Stephens watched as one man, trying to remove his cart from the blockade in St. Stephens Green, was shot dead by a rebel rifleman. "At that moment the Volunteers were hated," (Stephens, *The Insurrection in Dublin* 24).

But besides isolated events like this, and contrary to later accounts in the media vilifying the rebels, the real feelings of the suspicious Dublin citizenry toward the insurrection were indeterminate, and most people were tight-lipped. Three days into the uprising Stephens cautioned that it would be impossible to tell who the people were rooting for:

> Was the City for or against the Volunteers? Was it for the Volunteers, and yet against the rising? It is considered now (writing a day or two afterwards) that Dublin was entirely

against the Volunteers, but on the day of which I write no such certainty could be put forward. There was a singular reticence on the subject. Men met and talked volubly, but they said nothing that indicated a personal desire or belief. They asked for and exchanged the latest news, or, rather, rumour, and while expressions were frequent of astonishment at the suddenness and completeness of the occurrence, no expression of opinion for or against was anywhere formulated. (46–47)

Discretion was necessary between strangers, surely, because plain-clothes Volunteers and even plain-clothes government officials crawled Dublin's streets, but though Stephens endeavors to maintain an air of objectivity in *The Insurrection*, glimpses of a shallow and ingratiate citizenry—not unlike the Dubliners of *Here are the Ladies*—pop up here and there. In an early attempt to retake the General Post Office, British soldiers charged the building on horseback but were driven off by gunfire:

> In connection with this lancer charge at the Post Office it is said that the people, and especially the women, sided with the soldiers, and that the Volunteers were assailed by these women with bricks, bottles, sticks, to cries of:
> "Would you be hurting the poor men?"
> There were other angry ladies who threatened Volunteers, addressing them to this petrifying query:
> "Would you be hurting the poor horses?"
> Indeed, the best people in the world live in Dublin. (32)

While Stephens maintained a quiet dispensation to the cause of the Volunteers and judged some Dubliners base for choosing the side that would certainly come out on top, the immobility, the gun shots day and night between snipers in the Shelbourne Hotel and gunmen in the Green, the martial law and the curfews, the quick lack of food and other staples, and the looting of city shops, were all cause for animosity toward the rebels. But as the days went on and the Volunteers held their positions (a feat more incredible than their initial occupation of the city), Stephens detected a slight change in opinion. The English had arrived and made a stand, and yet the Volunteers remained. "There is almost a feeling of gratitude towards the Volunteers because they are holding out for a while," Stephens records, "for had they been beaten the first or second day the City would have been humiliated to the soul," (52). Augmenting this sentiment was the quick justice dealt to the rebels when caught. Some were executed on their knees in the street. Others had quick trials and given the death penalty. All the leaders of the Easter Rising were tried and executed within ten days of the insurrection. In the end, British justice did more to sway public opinion toward Irish Republicanism than any of the planners of the rebellion might have guessed. The failed insurrection became an important step toward the Irish Republic.

Both Stephens and Yeats wrote elegies for the patriots of the Easter Rising. In Stephens's "The Spring in Ireland, 1916" from his collection, *Green Branches*, the speaker implores that those who lost their lives in the rising be remembered with all the hopefulness of spring:

> Be green upon their graves, O happy Spring,
> For they were young and eager who are dead;
> Of all things that are young and quivering
> With eager life be they rememberéd:
> They move not here, they have gone to the clay,
> They cannot die again for liberty;
> Be they remembered of their land for aye;
> Green be their graves and green their memory.
>   (Stephens, "Spring" lines 27–34)

But it is Yeats's verse, "Easter 1916," a frequent inclusion in anthologies, which has become the most celebrated verse on the insurrection. A complex poem, it joins Easter and the resurrection of Christ with the imminent rise of the Irish state, especially in the refrain, "A terrible beauty is born." But it also conveys his sense of the damaging consequences of zealous nationalism— the bewildering "excess of love," expressing at the same time hopefulness:

> Was it needless death after all?
> For England may keep faith
> For all that is done and said.
> We know their dream; enough
> To know they dreamed and are dead;
> And what if excess of love
> Bewildered them till they died?
> I write it out in a verse—
> MacDonagh and MacBride
> And Connolly and Pearse
> Now and in time to be,
> Wherever green is worn,
> Are changed, changed utterly:
> A terrible beauty is born.
> (Yeats, *Easter 1916*, lines 67–80)

"Easter 1916" was written in late September of that year, time enough for the leaders of the Rising to be transformed from criminals into martyrs. Just three years later a majority of the MPs elected to Westminster refused to sit in the British House of Commons, forming instead the Dáil Éireann, the Irish Parliament, in that important cultural center, Leinster House. They issued a Declaration of Independence, but few in the international community paid any attention. It was only after a hard-fought war that dominion status was granted to the new Irish Free State in the Treaty of 1921, though neither side was content with the terms, and a civil war ensued between Pro-Treaty and Anti-Treaty factions. A new constitution in 1937 finally created the nation called Ireland out of the southern three-quarters of the island, though it remained a British Commonwealth until 1949. Even in the present day, Irish citizens have many of the same privileges within the United Kingdom that British citizens enjoy.

The First World War had the effect of a bulldozer on cultures around Europe and beyond. It changed English literature forever, and brought the Irish Literary Revival to a halt. But even when the war had ended, tumult took root in Ireland, especially in Dublin. The new Free State came with guerilla warfare and civil war. Despite the contributions of the figures of the Irish Literary Revival towards an Irish literature, and their work to establish Dublin as the center of the new culture—we would be hard-pressed to describe anything like a "literary Dublin" without them—many in later life left the city. Stephens's fame took him to America and, the Second World War (and his disapproval of Irish neutrality) took him to London, where he became a regular broadcaster for the BBC; he died following complications from a gastric operation, and was buried in London's Kingsbury Old Graveyard. Yeats, of course, bounced from western Ireland to eastern England, but he always considered Sligo his home. There he is buried per his wishes, "under bare Ben Bulben's head in Drumcliff churchyard," marked with the famous epitaph,

> Cast a cold Eye
> On Life, on Death.
> Horseman, pass by.

George Russell was perhaps the most attached to his city of residence, his door at 17 Rathgar Avenue famously unlocked even during the most volatile of Dublin days, but even he surprised acquaintances when he moved to England after his wife died. He passed away at a nursing home in Bournemouth, July 17, 1935, though his body was brought back to Dublin. His cortège to Mt. Jerome Cemetery was said to be more than a mile long, with eulogy given by author Frank O'Connor (Yeats declined) in the presence of personages the likes of patriot-politician Eamon de Valera. Republicans set ablaze Moore Hall in 1923, George Moore's ancestral home in County Mayo. He died in London ten years later. The trend continued with James Joyce, who lived and wrote mostly on the Continent, but wrote of Dublin like no one else before or since.

CHAPTER SEVEN

Dublin, Joyce, and *Ulysses*

There have probably been more words written about the relationship between James Joyce and Dublin than that of any other author and any other place. Because his writings confined themselves to Dublin, because he set his stories in specific places and those places were always important to the story, because he presented the city as he experienced it or imagined it experienced, often for the worse rather than the better, because he bid good riddance to Dublin but wrote longingly of it, and because Dublin figures so prominently in one of the most innovative, influential, and controversial books of the twentieth century, his *Ulysses*, scholars have obsessed over the question of Joyce and Dublin. Sentiments of love and hate for his hometown have been documented, analyzed, and overanalyzed. On the one hand, he ridiculed Yeats and Dublin's culturati, and was at best indifferent to nationalism during a nation's most volatile times. He was convinced that artistic and spiritual liberty lay beyond the paralysis of Dublin. On the other hand, he was aware that his self-imposed exile became, after *Ulysses*, a real one, and that his city would not welcome him back. Depictions of Dublin hung on the walls of his Paris apartment, and the turns of the Liffey were woven into the rug on its floor.

Joyce was born at 41 Brighton Square on February 2, 1882, probably in the first floor's master bedroom. The brick home still stands (as do, remarkably, almost all of young Joyce's many, many Dublin residences), marked by a plaque since 1964. He was the eldest (though not the first-born) in what would be a large family, and as such enjoyed the privileges of the oldest son in a moneyed family, even when the money vanished. He attended arguably the best boys' school in Ireland, Clongowes Wood College in County Kildare, and afterwards Belvedere College in Dublin. Both of these schools were run by Jesuits, and Joyce, deeply religious in his youth, entertained the notion of becoming a priest for a time, though by his middle teenage years he had fallen in love with literature—especially the plays of Ibsen—and opted to enter University College, Dublin, instead.

In college Joyce studied modern languages, and began to write essays and reviews of books and plays with some success. Of course, he had been exercising his hand in poetry, drama, and fiction, since he was a boy, though his earliest work was never published. Around this time, however, he began drafting *A Portrait of the Artist*, a short story, which was reworked into a long novel called *Stephen Hero*, a semi-autobiographical story of his Catholic upbringing. This he pared down with rejections from publishers over a period of ten years, until it was finally published in 1914 as *A Portrait of the Artist as a Young Man*.

Joyce almost left Dublin for good in January 1903, but he was only in Paris a few months when he received word that his mother was dying. She lingered until August of that year, leaving her nine children to the indifferent wiles of her drunken husband, John Joyce. James stayed in Dublin until the fall of 1904, during which time he met Oliver St. John Gogarty, the boisterous author, with whom he shared his most famous residence, Martello Tower, south of Dublin. He met Nora Barnacle, too, on Nassau Street, a chambermaid freshly fled from Galway, who, in love and without much else for her in Ireland, went with Joyce to Europe. They settled outside of Trieste, and later in Paris, moving to neutral Zürich during the First and Second World Wars. Joyce and Nora lived as husband and wife, producing two children during their life together, but—neither much for convention—did not marry until 1931, and then only out of legal necessity. Joyce went back to Ireland infrequently, and never after 1912.

DUBLINERS

By 1904, the short stories that ended up in *Dubliners* were appearing in the *Irish Homestead*, but readers' complaints about Joyce's portrayal of life in the city halted the series. Joyce spent years shopping for a publisher for his collection. Despite a dire need for cash, he squabbled with publishers over words and phrases they deemed inappropriate, which Joyce attributed to Dublin sanctimoniousness and London prudence. In his letters he tried to explain that the very objections to his stories (that they were, for one, bad for public morality) were his inspiration for writing about such lives in the first place. Particularly entertaining is Joyce's 1906 correspondence with the publisher Grant Richards, whose printer insisted on aggressively editing the manuscript even though Richards agreed to publish it. "O one-eyed printer!" Joyce wrote to Richard in May, "Why has he descended with his blue pencil, full of the Holy Ghost, upon these passages ...?" (Joyce, *Selected Letters of James Joyce* 82). In the same letter he restates his reason for writing of Dublin the way he did:

> My intention was to write a chapter of the moral history of my country and I chose Dublin for the scene because that city seemed to me the center of paralysis. I have tried to present it to the indifferent public under four of its aspects: childhood, adolescence, maturity and public life. The stories are arranged in this order. I have written it for the most part in a style of scrupulous meanness and with the conviction that he is a very bold man who dares to alter in the

presentment, still more to deform, what he has seen and heard. (*Selected Letters* 83)

The letters show Joyce's frustration. He felt that *Dubliners* was a work of mimesis, that through his 'scrupulous meanness,' his attention to detail, he has shown the 'paralysis' of Irish thought and culture. At length he was willing to compromise grudgingly on a few passages where he used the word 'bloody'—threatening that in omitting such details "Dubliners would seem to me like an egg without salt" (*Selected Letters* 84)—but elsewhere the details were too crucial to change. A letter to Richards in late May spelled out his lofty hopes for the stories:

> ... I believe that in composing my chapter of moral history in exactly the way I have composed it I have taken the first step towards the spiritual liberation of my country. Reflect for a moment on the history of the literature of Ireland as it stands at present written in the English language before you condemn this genial illusion of mine, which, after all, has at least served me in the office of a candlestick during the writing of the book. (88–89)

Richards's firm eventually published the book, but not for another eight years, in 1914. Joyce had similar trouble with another Dublin publisher, Maunsel & Co., which agreed to print the volume in 1909. But after three years no ground was gained, as George Roberts, who ran the firm, objected to Joyce's use of real place names among the usual plaints. When Joyce made what would be his last trip to Dublin in 1912 to rectify the situation once and for all, he discovered that Roberts had destroyed the typeset, inspiring the vilification of Roberts and theocracy in his poem, "Gas from a Burner."

ULYSSES

On an earlier visit to Dublin in 1909, Joyce visited with an old school acquaintance, Vincent Cosgrave, who shows up as the character named Lynch in *A Portrait of the Artist as a Young Man*. Whether it was because Cosgrave was unhappy with his portrayal in what was then *Stephen Hero*, as some suggest, or for different reasons altogether, Cosgrave claimed to have seduced Nora Barnacle while she and Joyce were courting back in 1904.

Ulysses and Censorship

Before Sylvia Beach famously published *Ulysses* in Paris in 1922, Joyce's modernist masterpiece had been appearing serially in a small Greenwich Village periodical called *The Little Review*, beginning in 1918. When in 1920 the two women who ran the publication printed the climactic ending of the Nausikaa episode, the Secretary of the Society for the Prevention of Vice, John Sumner, took the publishers to court, where the book was declared obscene and the women fined. The U.S. Postal Service intercepted copies of the magazine and burned them.

Thus banned, U.S. Customs officials were able to keep most copies of *Ulysses* out of the country, but were powerless against the praise and intrigue that crossed the Atlantic almost immediately after Beach's Shakespeare & Co. imprint. Smuggled copies and bootlegs began to appear, fetching prices as high as $50.

Then in 1933 Bennett Cerf, who headed up Random House, thought a loophole in the Tariff Act of 1930 allowing single copies of even banned books into the country for collectors might support a case to lift the ban on *Ulysses*. He ordered a copy, which was seized (as he expected), setting up the trial in which federal judge John Woolsey would rule whether or not Joyce's book was obscene. Woolsey took the book with him on vacation and read it in a month. His decision in early December 1933 to lift the ban on *Ulysses* was based on the literary merit of the book as a whole—not on whether the controversial parts were too obscene—and remains a landmark case in U.S. censorship law.

A wreck, Joyce ran to another old friend's house, J.F. Byrne, with whom Joyce attended Belvedere and University College, the character "Cranly" of *A Portrait*. At his home on 7 Eccles Street, Byrne managed to convince Joyce that Cosgrave had made up the story, but Joyce was struck by his brush with cuckoldry. When he set out to write the story of Leopold Bloom and his adulterous wife Molly the next year, he made the brick three-storey at 7 Eccles Street their home.

Joyce wrote *Ulysses* for Nora, setting all the events of the novel on one day, June 16, 1904, the day of their first date. It is an understatement to describe the book as dense. It is divided into eighteen unnamed episodes, each alluding to an event in Homer's *Odyssey*, and it features the wanderings Leopold Bloom as Odysseus, his wife Molly Bloom as Penelope, and his quasi-son Stephen Dedalus as Telemachus, along with hundreds of other correspondences. But Joyce has only begun. Each chapter is told from a different point of view, in a different style, all with intent. Each chapter refers to distinct colors, symbols, and sensations. Each embodies a branch of human knowledge. Each characterizes a different organ in the human body. Moreover, there are countless puzzles hidden in the text, many of which remain unsolved, like the identity of the Man in Macintosh who appears at Paddy Dignam's funeral, what Bloom wrote in the sand at Sandymount, and the reason Bloom's furniture is rearranged when he arrives home.

Published, finally, by Sylvia Beach in Paris, 1922, it took some time for Dubliners to accept Joyce and his book. *Ulysses* was banned in the United States and Britain until the 1930s, and while never officially banned in Ireland, copies would have been difficult to come by. But ever since June 14, 15, and 16, 1954—fifty years to the date of the events of the novel—Joyceans have been welcomed to the city for Bloomsday, when devotees follow the winding paths of Leopold Bloom and Stephen Dedalus around Dublin, doing what they did, eating what they ate, and saying what they said. There are walking tours, readings from the book, lectures on Joyce miscellanea, exhibits to attend, and play-actors to watch. So important is *Ulysses* to the history of literature that, for admirers who cannot make it to Dublin in June, Bloomsday celebrations are held in cities from Tokyo to New York.

If *Ulysses* is complex, *Finnegans Wake*, Joyce's last book, is inscrutable. Written in a sort of punning language, it was several years before serious academics cracked some of the plot. Readers are easily frustrated without a guide, and careful study is required to appreciate the novel. It, too, concerns Dublin, particularly the neighborhood of Chapelizod, and in fact contains many throwbacks to fellow Dubliner Joseph Sheridan Le Fanu and his *House by the Churchyard*. Many of the same characters show up, and Joyce variously summons Le Fanu's classic with "In the church by the hearseyard," "the old house by the churpelizod," and "De oud huis bij de kerkegaard," among others. Humphrey Chimpden Earwicker, whose dream is *Finnegans Wake*, lived in that selfsame house by the churchyard where Le Fanu set his story, marked today by a plaque.

There are many more Joycean connections in Chapelizod, just as hundreds of Dublin locales contribute to his *Dubliners* stories, and thousands of Dublin specifics are included in the whole of the Joycean canon. Yet in all of his works, Joyce wrote Dublin as he lived it and as he remembered it. That most of the *Dubliners* stories are set in the city's northeast side is no coincidence: this is the Dublin Joyce knew when his family moved within the city limits. *A Portrait*, being largely autobiographical, gathers many of the places in Dublin where Joyce grew to maturity. Thus, the character of his work makes it possible to trace the most salient places in Joyce's fiction through a survey of his Dublin life.

THE JOYCE FAMILY

James Joyce's father, John Stanislaus Joyce, was from a landed and established Catholic family in Cork, one that even boasted relation to the Liberator, Daniel O'Connell, but the considerable fortune with which John Joyce began adulthood was lost entirely in the course of James's youth. At twenty-one, John Joyce had properties in Cork earning £300 per year, and a sum of £1,000 given to him by his grandfather. He studied medicine in Cork but took it lightly, and set off to fight for the French in the Franco-Prussian War when his mother interceded, taking her twenty-five-year-old son to Dublin.

John Joyce's financial undoing began when he met Henry Alleyne, who had been running a successful distillery in Chapelizod, then a distinct little village about three miles outside the city. Alleyne invited Joyce to join the company. Investing £500, John Joyce was made secretary of the company, a position which collected a salary of £300 a year. The "still that was the mill," as Joyce calls it in *Finnegans Wake*, did well, supplying spirits to stores directly and shipping hundreds of thousands of gallons of its signature "Dublin Whiskey" to London and beyond. But when John Joyce took a peek at the books, he discovered that Alleyne had been embezzling from the company. He made his findings available to the board, which decided to close the distillery. Alleyne disappeared. Joyce lost his job and his initial investment. One wall of the old distillery remains in Chapelizod today, but the house next door in which his father lived—and where Mr. Duffy of the *Dubliners* story "A Painful Case" resided—was razed in the 1970s.

At least Joyce met his future wife through the distillery. The daughter of a wine and spirits merchant, Mary Jane ("May") Murray was just nineteen to Joyce's twenty-nine when they met, and despite prohibitions from her father, who knew John Joyce to be taken to drink, they married the next year, in 1880. They moved into lodgings at 47 Northumberland Avenue in the suburb of Dun Laoghaire, and John landed a job as Collector of Rates in Dublin, earning a considerable salary of £500 a year. May became pregnant soon after, but the child, a boy, lived only a few weeks. The pain of such a loss probably prompted their move to Rathgar, 41 Brighton Square, where James Joyce was born. It was a newer home, only five years old, but then all the houses in Rathgar were relatively new, the suburb only developed since the 1860s. After James was born John Joyce mortgaged the first of his Cork properties for extra money, a financial move he repeated in the next dozen years whenever money was short, until he had mortgaged them all. Eventually, mounting debts forced him to sell what was left of his Cork holdings, the trip to Cork chronicled in *A Portrait.*

JOYCE'S EARLY YEARS

When Joyce was two years old the family moved to Rathmines, a little closer to the city center. Three more children were born to the Joyces at 23 Castlewood Avenue, with three more mortgages in Cork. They were still very well off during this time, living in fine homes in middle class, professional neighborhoods, their frequent moves precipitated by John Joyce's domestic wanderlust rather than financial necessity. Rather than buying, renting a home made sense to many middle class families in Dublin at that time, since rent was low and housing plentiful. But it seems John Joyce was reluctant to stay in one place for long, and this was the primary reason the Joyces did not settle down when they had the chance. Their next move to Bray, in County Wicklow, about thirteen miles outside the city, was made by John Joyce to distance himself from his in-laws, who would have to take a train to see them in their oceanside home at 1 Martello Terrace. This, too, was a great house in a well-to-do neighborhood, with the Joyces surrounded by friends. Both John Kelley, the basis for Mr. Casey in *A Portrait* and William O'Connell, John Joyce's uncle (called 'Uncle Charles' in the book) lived with the Joyce family in Bray. Mr. Joyce had not yet drunk away their livelihood (though he would) and they still afforded servants in the household, including the draconian governess Mrs. Conway, who figures as 'Dante' (a child's pronunciation of 'Auntie') in *A Portrait.* It was here at their home in Bray that the fierce fight over Parnell takes place during Christmas dinner, 1891. Charles Parnell had made tremendous advances toward Irish Home Rule until a divorce scandal generated pressure from the Irish Catholic clergy, among other factions, to oust him from parliamentary leadership in 1890. Parnell's tiring campaign to recapture the Home Rule party through 1891 saw him dead in October of that year. Thus the Christmas scene at the Joyce household only months after Parnell's death ends with Mr. Casey sobbing "We have had too much God in Ireland. Away with God!" and Dante, a pious Catholic once spurned in love, screaming back, "Devil out of hell! We won! We crushed him to death! Fiend!" (*Portrait* 39).

Young Joyce, then just nine years old and enrolled at Clongowes Wood College in County Kildare since he was six, was home at the time for Christmas break. He was so young when entering the school that his father was able to make arrangements to pay half the usual tuition for his son, but that year his alcoholism cost him his job as Collector of Rates, and even this reduced tuition was a financial burden after December, 1892. Earlier in 1892 the family moved to a more affordable home in Blackrock at 23 Carysfort Avenue, where James enjoyed the large back garden and (less so) nearby Blackrock Park, where his father's friend Mike Flynn made him run track like an athlete through the summer, described in the opening pages of *A Portrait*'s Book II. Two daughters were born at this house, called "Leoville," making ten children in all. (May Joyce bore fifteen children in her lifetime, but only ten survived infancy. Georgie, their third son, died tragically of typhoid fever at the age of fourteen.) A plaque denotes Joyce's time here, however short: again they moved in the winter of 1893. It was evident to Joyce, now, that something was amiss. The flight from Blackrock was hasty, and Dante and William O'Connell were not with them at their new address, 29 Hardwicke Street. Leveled in the fifties for block housing, this is one of Joyce's few Dublin residences that has not survived. They stayed only a few months, though Joyce would remember the boarding house down the road at 4 Hardwicke Street, setting his *Dubliners* story "The Boarding House" there.

Their next home at 14 Fitzgibbon Street was Joyce's first chance to explore Dublin, realizing then, as he tells it in *A*

Portrait, "the vastness and strangeness of life" (*Portrait* 66). Used to suburban areas like Blackrock, his experiences in the city began with his "circling timidly round the neighboring square," that is, Mountjoy Square, "but when he had made a skeleton map of the city in his mind he followed boldly one of its central lines until he reached the customshouse" (66). His route was Gardiner Street South to the Custom House and beyond to the bustling docks, a scene quite strange to a boy used to the sublime setting of Clongowes, or the open spaces and ocean views of Bray and Blackrock.

> He passed unchallenged among the docks and along the quays wondering at the multitude of corks that lay bobbing on the surface of the water in a thick yellow scum, at the crowds of quay porters and the rumbling carts and the ill-dressed bearded policemen. (66)

In 1893 Joyce was able to resume his Jesuit education thanks to the good graces of a Father Conmee, onetime rector at Clongowes who was now serving as the Prefect of Studies at Belvedere College. John Joyce, who, if little else, had a knack for negotiation (especially with creditors and landlords), and persuaded Conmee to allow James and his younger brother Stanislaus into Belvedere at no cost. Joyce studied there for five years until his graduation in 1898, excelling in academics. He won several cash prizes for his essays, and even placed thirteenth in Ireland for mathematics. Belvedere remains at 6 Great Denmark Street, though a few of the more memorable Belvedere locations in *A Portrait* are gone: the gymnasium where Dedalus donned a beard and wrinkles to play the schoolmaster in *Vice Versa* was torn down in the seventies; and the chapel in which he was stricken with the fear of God in observance of Saint Francis's day is now a part of the science department. But a stone's throw from Belvedere at no. 35 North Great George's Street, an eighteenth century Georgian townhouse is the modern-day headquarters of the James Joyce Centre, dedicated to the author's life and work. The Centre features an array of Joyceana, though its one permanent exhibit is the original front door to the house at 7 Eccles Street, which was demolished in 1982. Guided walking tours of Joyce's Dublin leave from here three days a week.

During Joyce's time at Belvedere the family only moved twice, to a house in Drumcondra first, and then to 17 North Richmond Street, an area heavily represented in the stories in *Dubliners*. His "Araby" was in this house, on this street, but the story was imaginary, of a boy enamored by a neighborhood girl he plans to meet at the Araby bazaar, held historically in Dublin in May, 1984. In the tale, the boy imagines the rude business of Dublin against his romantic purposes:

> On Saturday evenings when my aunt went marketing I had to go to carry some of the parcels. We walked through the flaring streets, jostled by drunken men and bargaining women, amid the curses of labourers, the shrill litanies of shop-boys who stood on guard by the barrels of pigs' cheeks, the nasal chanting of street-singers, who sang a come-all-you about O'Donovan Rossa, or a ballad about the troubles in our native land. These noises converged in a single sensation of life for me: I imagined that I bore my chalice safely through a throng of foes. (Joyce, *Dubliners* 31)

In the end the distractions of Dublin are his foes. The night of the bazaar, the boy waits for his uncle's return for money to pay the admission, but, out drinking, his uncle comes home too late. With no power over his own fate, the boy fails to meet the girl at the right time—one instance of "paralysis" in Dublin, here of Irish adolescence. "An Encounter" draws heavily on Joyce's memory of North Richmond Street too, the Indian battles he describes occurring in the garden of a neighbor's house, no. 20. Later in the story, Joyce describes a brush he and his brother Stanislaus had with a pederast. In *My Brother's Keeper*, an unparalleled insight into the author, Stanislaus Joyce relates that this was one of the stories that made publishers anxious. Joyce's reassurance that it was a factual account was to no avail.

Providing much ambience for his work, it must be said that North Richmond Street and other neighborhoods in northeast Dublin are, for the most part, the Dublin of James Joyce. The city south of the Liffey and the surrounding suburbs—then and now—are of the middle and professional classes. Far more interesting to Joyce than the Georgian monuments of Temple Bar and Merrion Square are the blue collar districts of Dublin's north side. Here is the "moral history" of the Irish.

Joyce graduated from Belvedere in 1898, deciding, to his mother's dismay, to attend University College in St. Stephens Green instead of taking the divine office. As one might expect, he did well here, too, and remains among the most important figures associated with the College. A plaque outside Newman House recognizes the school's founder, Cardinal John Henry Newman, the nineteenth century poet Gerard Manley Hopkins, who taught here, and James Joyce. The author's statue has stood in the neighboring Green since its erection in 1982. The Joyces moved to six different addresses in the four years James studied at the university, always under the threat of eviction, since by now John Joyce considered rent low on his list of priorities. Their residences during this time were mostly in the vicinity of Fairview, including homes at 29 Windsor Avenue, 13 Richmond Avenue (now demolished), and 8 Royal Terrace (now Inverness Road), dubbed by Joyce "Royal Terror, Fearview." From each of these young Joyce walked every morning, past the swamps that have since been cultivated to form Fairview Park, south across the Liffey, to school in St. Stephen's Green. East of Fairview is the site of *A Portrait*'s climax at the mouth of the Liffey in Dollymount, where Stephen glimpses the city pathetically, as reluctant to develop its own *raison d'être* as it had been when it welcomed the Vikings:

A veiled sunlight lit up faintly the grey sheet of water where the river was embayed. In the distance along the course of the slowflowing Liffey slender masts flecked the sky and, more distant still, the dim fabric of the city lay prone in haze. Like a scene on some vague arras, old as man's weariness, the image of the seventh city of christendom was visible to him across the timeless air, no older nor more weary nor less patient of subjection than in the days of the thingmote. (*Portrait* 167)

(The exact location of the Thingmote, a sort of Viking town hall, is the subject of contention, but tradition holds that it operated on what is now College Green.) Dismayed with the sight of the stagnant city, Stephen envisions the "Europe of strange tongues and valleyed and woodbegirt and citadelled and of entrenched and marshalled races" across the Irish Sea (167), and realizes he should leave and live. His epiphany materializes on the nearby beach in the form of an alluring girl, her back to Dublin, looking out over the ocean.

The character Little Chandler of "A Little Cloud" shares Stephen's sentiments. For a short while he fancies himself a poet, musing that he could leave and become someone. "For the first time his soul revolted against the dull inelegance of Capel Street. There was no doubt about: if you wanted to succeed you had to go away. You could do nothing in Dublin" (*Dubliners* 73). Sadly, Little Chandler is trapped. James Joyce left Dublin when he could.

One of Joyce's last lodgings before he left Ireland is probably his most famous. Home to the James Joyce Museum since Bloomsday, 1962, the old Martello Tower in Sandycove, nine miles south of Dublin, was built by the British in 1804 to defend against possible attack from Napoleon's forces. Joyce's friend, Oliver St. John Gogarty, arranged to let the vacant tower from the British War Department in June 1904, for £8 a year, and Joyce joined him in September. His stay was less than a week, hastened by his crazy roommates who took one night to firing a revolver within the tower's eight-foot thick walls. Irate, Joyce left the country a month later. Of course, it is the tower's place in the opening chapter of *Ulysses*—not Joyce's six-day stay—that made it famous as the James Joyce Tower. Today its round room is furnished as it was when Joyce lived there, and the museum's collection on the ground floor contains some of Joyce's personal effects, letters, and other relics from *Ulysses*.

Ulysses has made famous many Dublin sites beyond Sandycove. Guided walking tours of the Dublin in *Ulysses* can be arranged at the James Joyce Centre, 35 North Great George's Street, on Tuesday, Thursday, and Saturday afternoons. As a primer, what follows is a chapter-by-chapter breakdown of the Dublin landmarks in this masterpiece of twentieth century fiction.

* * *

Episode 1: Telemachus

Everything is important in *Ulysses*, but the importance given to place is exceptional.

This tower is one of many that dot the Irish coastline, employed by Joyce as symbols of the English in Ireland, as hard to evict as Penelope's suitors. That the novel begins with Stephen Dedalus a considerable distance from Dublin corresponds to Telemachus's separation from Odysseus, and, with tensions rising between Dedalus and his obnoxious roommate Buck Mulligan (a Joyce jab at Gogarty), by the end of the scene Stephen decides to begin his Telemachia, landing him, in the space of a day, at 7 Eccles Street. But more than the blasphemer Mulligan has Stephen leaving. There is mention of the sorry state of Irish art—to Stephen, analogous to "the cracked lookingglass of a servant" (6)—such that Stephen's journey will be a spiritual one, away from the messy history represented in the Martello Tower. The nearby Forty Foot bathing pool where Mulligan plunges continues to host nude bathers year-round, though the sign that once read "FORTY FOOT GENTLEMEN ONLY" is long gone—the baths have been patronized by both sexes since the 1970s.

Episode 2: Nestor

About one mile south of Joyce's tower along Dalkey Avenue, a house called "Summerfield" is the site of Mr. Deasy's school, called Clifton School in 1904 when Joyce taught there for a short time. The schoolhouse is still in business, though on the other side of the building, and the stone porch remains where Stephen is paid by Deasy, the anti-Semitic Nestor. The "lions couchant" on Summerfield's gates have not survived.

Episode 3: Proteus

Having just been paid, Dedalus can afford the train fare north to the Lansdowne Road Station, not far from James Joyce's lodgings in May and June, 1904, at 60 Shelbourne Road. New roads in the vicinity make it difficult to determine Stephen's exact route to the strand. The beach too has changed, the sand perhaps a hundred yards southeast from where it was a hundred years ago, a homage to the episode's namesake, the gloomy, shifting sea-god. Stephen's peregrinations here—"Am I walking into eternity along Sandymount Strand?" (31)—take him to a point of rocks south of Pigeonhouse Road and perhaps further out to the Poolbeg lighthouse, when the rising tide forces him back through Irishtown toward central Dublin.

Episode 4: Calypso

Leopold Bloom's day begins with a hankering for a pork kidney at 7 Eccles Street (see above), no more but once across the street from no. 76. A plaque at the Mater Private Hospital nearby memorializes the site. Like Odysseus he has been ensnared by the witch Calypso, not the woman he married—his wife Molly having been unfaithful to him with at least one man, Blazes Boylan. Molly and Bloom have not had an amorous marriage since their infant son, Rudy, died ten years earlier. The pork kidney he wants (significant because Bloom is of Jewish ancestry) takes him down Dorset Street Upper, past Larry O'Rourke's pub on the corner (nos. 72–73, now a bar called The Snug) and St. Joseph's National School (now called

St. Raphael's House, at 81–84) to Dlugacz's, the butcher, a fictious place. Back at the house, he delivers to bed-bound Molly breakfast and a letter from her lover, and after burning his own breakfast in the basement kitchen, he leaves to walk the quays.

Episode 5: The Lotus Eaters

Joyce does not explain how Bloom got to Sir John Rogerson's Quay at the beginning of the episode, but the easiest route across the Liffey would have been the nearby Butt Bridge. His intention is to bathe this morning in Tara Street before Paddy Dignam's funeral, but a more intriguing errand has him dallying at the coal yards and warehouses of Lime Street, surreptitiously approaching the Westland Row Post Office (once at the train station). Where Hanover Street becomes Townsend he makes a left onto Lombard Street, passing Nichol's undertakers, still operating. Crossing Great Brunswick Street, Bloom loops in front of the Grosvenor Hotel, which used to be next to the railway bridge. Across the street, the old doorway to the Westland Row Post Office is now an entrance to the train station's booking offices. Inside, Bloom retrieves the letter from his secret pen pal, Martha Clifford; the lumberyard where he hovers over her sultry words is no longer there, but St. Andrew's church, through which Bloom passes from the rear and out onto Westland Row, stands as it has since the 1830s.

Walking down Westland Row toward Lincoln Place, Bloom would have passed the birthplace of Oscar Wilde, at no. 21, though Joyce makes no mention of it. Just ahead, Bloom stops at F.W. Sweny's to order Molly's lotion, where he also buys some lemon soap. "Chemists rarely move," he thinks (68). The sign reading "Sweny" still hangs above M.F. Quinn's drugstore on Lincoln Place. By now Bloom will never get to the baths in Tara Street and make it to Newbridge Avenue for the Dignam cortège, and while we are never sure where he does take his hasty soak, a hint in the "Ithaca" episode suggests it was at the Turkish and Warm Baths, 11 Leinster Street. Those baths are now part of an office block, but *en route*, the last building on the right where Lincoln Place merges with Leinster Street used to be Finn's Hotel. Here Nora Barnacle was employed as a chambermaid before she met James Joyce. It has not been a hotel since 1947, but the name is still visible in white paint above the Bagel and Juice Depot.

Episode 6: Hades

Paddy Dignam's funeral procession begins at his home, 9 New-bridge Avenue, Sandymount, and ends in Glasnevin Cemetery, its route well documented in *Ulysses*. Those who plan to walk the path should allow two hours' time.

Glasnevin, called officially Prospect Cemetery, was one of Daniel O'Connell's victories. Since the rigid Penal Laws forbade Catholic ritual in public, and Dublin's Catholics had no ceme-teries of their own, they had been forced to conduct an abbrevi-ated ritual in Protestant cemeteries. By 1824 O'Connell had won the legal battle, and Glasnevin saw its first burial in 1832. When O'Connell died in 1847, the large round tower at the cemetery's center was prepared for his remains at the suggestion of the antiquarian George Petrie. Joyce's parents are buried here: at last count around 1.5 million were buried within the ceme-tery's 120 acres.

Episode 7: Aeolus

Mourning coaches have brought the attendees of Dignam's funeral back to central Dublin. Much of this episode takes place at the offices of the *Freeman's Journal*, 4–8 Prince's Street, but the paper has since become the *Irish Independent* and the *Evening Herald*, across from the General Post Office. Joyce makes mention of Nelson's Pillar as "the heart of the Hibernian metropolis," famous for its onetime function as a hub for Dublin's trams, but blown to bits by the I.R.A. in 1966. Nelson's Pillar has been replaced by the Spire of Dublin, in the center of the city's main thoroughfare, O'Connell Street (for-merly Sackville Street). (The subject of some derision from Dubliners, "the Spike" goes by other formulations of Irish wit, such as the "Stiletto in the Ghetto," and the "Erection at the Intersection.") Stephen Dedalus has followed the same route taken by the cortège from Sandymount into the center of town, stopped to visit the Post Office in College Green, but narrowly missed meeting Bloom at the newspaper.

The Oval, the pub where Simon Dedalus and others go for drinks, remains at 78 Middle Abbey Street. Stephen Dedalus and his companions are in front of Mooney's pub, 1 Lower Abbey Street, when the episode ends. The establishment is now part of a bank, but above its glass-encased doorway is still inscribed "Mooney & Co. Ltd. Wines & Spirits."

Episode 8: Lestrygonians

It is lunchtime, and Bloom wants to eat somewhere on his way to the National Library. His route is one of the easiest in *Ulysses* to follow. Southbound, he feeds the birds at O'Connell Bridge, crosses Aston Quay toward the Ballast Office (called Ballast House after its 1979 reconstruction), past the offices of the *Irish Times*, under the statue of Thomas Moore and his "roguish finger." He is nearly run down by Æ on a bicycle in front of the Provost's House on Grafton Street, and, crossing Nassau, he looks at binoculars in the window of Yeates & Son, which has moved from the corner.

> Grafton Street gay with housed awnings lured his senses. Muslin prints, silk, dames and dowagers, jingle of harnesses, hoofthuds lowringing in the baking causeway. Thick feet that woman has in the white stockings. Hope the rain mucks them up on her. Country bred chewbacon. All the beef to the heels were in. Always gives a woman clumsy feet. Molly looks out of plumb.
>
> He passed, dallying, the windows of Brown Thomas, silk mercers. Cascades of ribbons. Flimsy China silks. A tilted urn poured from its mouth a flood of bloodhued poplin: lustrous blood. The huguenots brought that here. (137–138)

Brown Thomas moved to the other side of the street in the 90s. At the Marks and Spencer complex—then Combridge's—he cuts right into Duke Street. Starving, he steps in the Burton Hotel at 18 Duke Street, but he is so disgusted by the "dirty eaters" that he has to leave. It is only one kind of cannibal in this episode of eating. The Burton closed a long time ago, though whether this came about from the quality of its food is not known. Bloom backtracks to Davy Byrne's pub, at 21 Duke Street, for his famous lunch: a gorgonzola sandwich and burgundy. Visitors today won't have any potted meat to stare at, and its sparkling interior would have been unrecognizable to Bloom, but the pub has nevertheless embraced its Joycean connection. After lunch he crosses Dawson Street, walks the length of Molesworth past the Freemason's Hall, and is heading up Kildare to the library when he spies the straw hat of Blazes Boylan coming his way. In a frenzy he ducks into the National Gallery; Bloom had wanted to check on the anatomy of the statues in the foyer, anyway. The Venuses once in the National Gallery's rotunda have long since been replaced with Celtic crosses and other relics by fastidious officials.

Episode 9: Scylla and Charybdis

A library card is required to enter the upstairs Reading Room, where, in an office to the right, Stephen Dedalus, John Eglinton, and Æ discuss literature, until Æ has to leave to attend the business of the *Irish Homestead*. After he departs the biggest names of Dublin literature are dropped regarding a party that everyone seems to be attending, except Dedalus. Bloom brushes past on the Library's portico, Odysseus navigating the whirling maelstrom of Charybdis.

Episode 10: The Wandering Rocks

The fragments in this section detail the wanderings of a number of characters all over the city, but mostly in south Dublin and never north of Ormond Quay. Bloom's only task is rifling through the books under the Merchants' Arch in Temple Bar, perhaps outside Francis Fitzgerald's shop, no. 1 Merchants' Arch, looking for something pornographic for Molly. Blazes Boylan buys fruit for Bloom's wife at a store called Thornton's on Grafton Street, now Dunne's Stores. Stephen meets Artifoni at the gates of Trinity College, walks north to Fleet Street and makes a right into Bedford Row, heading for a bookstore called Clohissey's that used to be at nos. 10–11, now a garage. He bumps into his sister here, who after waiting for hours in front of Dillon's auction rooms on Bachelor's Walk (where Bloom saw her on his way to lunch) finally met and got a few pennies from her father. Simon Dedalus continues west along the Quay to the Ormond Hotel.

Episode 11: Sirens

Remodeled, of course, the Ormond Hotel at 8 Upper Ormond Quay pays tribute to its place in *Ulysses* with its "Sirens Lounge," and a plaque outside remembers the connection. Many of the characters in *Ulysses* are lured to this hotel, never to be heard from again.

Episode 12: The Cyclops

Historically, many legal matters from the Criminal Court were settled at Barney Kiernan's pub, 8–10 Little Britain Street, now a hairdresser's shop. Here Bloom encounters "the citizen," a myopic (or is it cycloptic?) nationalist with an angry hate for anything that does not bleed green. Anxious for a fight, the citizen rallies other patrons in the pub to attack Bloom for his Jewish background. Bloom boldly defends himself, prompting the citizen to hurl a biscuit pan his way, like the Cyclops tossing a boulder at Odysseus and his men in flight. It is a mighty toss, but the tinbox lands harmlessly in Little Britain Street.

Episode 13: Nausikaa

In Sandymount again, Bloom has just finished paying his respects to Mrs. Paddy Dignam, the sun setting as he makes his way from Newbridge Avenue to the beach.

The summer evening had begun to fold the world in its mysterious embrace. Far away in the west the sun was setting and the last glow of all too fleeting day lingered lovingly on sea and strand, on the proud promontory of dear old Howth guarding as ever the waters of the bay, on the weedgrown rocks along Sandymount shore and, last but not least, on the quiet church whence there streamed forth at times upon the stillness the voice of prayer to her who is in her pure radiance a beacon ever to the stormtossed heart of man, Mary, star of the sea. (284)

Bloom and Stephen wander symmetrically in *Ulysses*, Bloom being in the same place this evening that Stephen had been this morning. In the hundred years since Joyce's setting, a fair amount of acreage has been taken back from the sea and developed, so it is difficult to imagine where Bloom eyes Gerty MacDowell and where he would have scratched his mysterious message in the sand, but it is surely somewhere between the Star of the Sea Church on Sandymount Road and the shore, because the two can hear the Benediction from the church in the background during their brief exchange.

Joyce borrowed Gerty's companions, Edy Boardman and Cissy Caffrey and the twins, from North Richmond Street. The Boardmans lived across the street from the Joyces, at no. 1, and the Caffreys next door at 6 Richmond Parade.

Episode 14: Oxen of the Sun

At the National Maternity Hospital on Holles Street, wherein the sacred miracle of birth is still taking place, Bloom visits Mrs. Purefoy who has endured three days of labor. He bumps into Stephen Dedalus, drinking for hours now, and some medical students who, if not yet drunk, at least pay no respect to their surroundings, singing bawdy songs and speaking with nonchalance of birth defects and whoring. Remembering his son Rudy, who lived only eleven days, Bloom is annoyed at the revelry taking place in the hospital, as profane as Odysseus's crew slaughtering Apollo's sacred oxen. After taking in drinks at Burke's, now a flower shop on the corner of Holles and Fenian, Stephen and his friend Lynch make for Westland Row Station to catch a train for Dublin's red light district. Bloom follows.

Episode 15: Circe

Called Monto by most, Joyce's nighttown was swept clean by Free State law enforcement in 1925. Girls were taken away and cared for, buildings were razed and rebuilt, and the names of some of the streets were changed to shed old associations. North from the Custom House, Montgomery Street (from which was derived 'Monto') is now Foley Street; Gloucester Street became Sean McDermott; Tyrone Street, where Bella Cohen's famous brothel was housed at no. 82, is now Railroad Street (before Tyrone it was Mecklenburgh, as in the novel); and Mabbot Street became Corporation Street, until, quite recently, it was renamed James Joyce Street. The irony of naming a street in what used to be the worst part of Dublin after the man who immortalized it would not have been lost on Mr. Joyce.

Amiens Street Station looks much the same, but now it is called Connolly Station. From here Stephen and Lynch embark into phantasmal nighttown, across Amiens Street and down Talbot, making a right onto Mabbot (James Joyce) Street, another right on Tyrone (Railroad) Street to Bella's brothel, which Joyce erroneously numbers 81 (it was no. 82). Bloom should have been with them but he neglected to get off the train at Amiens Station and had to backtrack from the next stop, Killester. Now well behind them, he follows their route. He stops at a number of establishments along the way, but only Olhausen's, 72 Talbot Street, has survived under the same name in the same place. Finally, in the famous whorehouse, Bloom and Stephen reunite. Soon, at the corner of Beaver Street and modern-day Railroad Street, the drunken and nightmare-afflicted Stephen is put down by two British soldiers. Bloom comes to his aid, dispersing the crowd and turning away the police. Bending over the incoherent Stephen, Bloom envisions his dead son, Rudy, bejeweled.

Episode 16: Eumaeus

Bloom and Stephen's route from the corner at Beaver Street to the cabman's shelter at Butt Bridge is easy, and a remarkable number of landmarks on their trip have survived. Dan Bergin's at 46 Amiens Street is now called Lloyd's; the Signal House, just before the railway bridge, is now Cleary's; the North Star Hotel still operates across from the train station; the Dock Tavern is called Master Mariner's, a storefront from the morgue, still standing. But gone, unfortunately, is the cabman's shelter under the railway bridge, where most of the scene takes place.

Episode 17: Ithaca

The way home is laid out in plain, catechistic words in the opening lines of the episode, roughly a reversal of the route walked by Stephen Dedalus when he leaves at the end of *A Portrait*. At the door to 7 Eccles Street, Bloom realizes that he has forgotten his key. Just weeks before *Ulysses* went to press, Joyce wrote to his aunt in Dublin to check on a detail:

> Is it possible for an ordinary person to climb over the area railings of no 7 Eccles street, either from the path or the steps, lower himself from the lowest part of the railings till his feet are within 2 feet or 3 of the ground and drop unhurt. I saw it done myself but by a man of rather athletic build. (*Selected Letters* 286)

Bloom does just that, letting Stephen in through the front door. They have cocoa, talk, and urinate in the back garden. Stephen declines Bloom's invitation to stay for the night, and Joyce never reveals where he goes. Inside Bloom finds his furniture rearranged and some books placed upside-down on the shelves. Crawling into bed, he finds himself at peace with Molly's infidelity.

Episode 18: Penelope

The eight sentences of Molly Bloom's stream-of-consciousness conclusion to *Ulysses* circumscribe her day, her previous boyfriends, her girlhood, and increasingly in the episode, her husband. Her last thoughts are of Bloom's marriage proposal to her in Howth, where flowers have grown since peat was carted up to the bare rock more than 150 years ago.

> ... and I thought well as well him as another and then I asked him with my eyes to ask again yes and then he asked me would I yes to say yes my mountain flower and first I put my arms around him yes and drew him down to me so he could feel my breasts all perfume yes and his heart was going like mad and yes I said yes I will Yes. (*Ulysses* 643–644)

CHAPTER EIGHT

Independence

In the 1920s Dublin lost two of the finest playwrights it would ever produce. Sean O'Casey, a child of Dublin's slums who was able to reproduce the lives of the urban poor like no one else, was practically run out of town by the Dublin public. *The Plough and the Stars*, with its poor portrayal of the Irish Citizen Army, was salt in the battle wounds of the nascent Irish state. Samuel Beckett, born a generation later, could not be persuaded from the avant-gardism of the Continent. There he befriended and worked closely with Joyce (but was not his secretary, contrary to a still-popular rumor), and made Paris his home. The Foxrock-born author's reputation rests on his play *Waiting for Godot*, which puzzled audiences in 1952, but soon left (and still leaves) playgoers teary-eyed with its exposition of the incomprehensible human condition. Beckett attended Trinity College, and taught there for a short while.

In the turbulent, sometimes violent, Dublin of the 1920s, the men who insisted on Irish liberty nothing short of complete sovereignty were jostling for power with those who sought compromise. Troubled by the ongoing civil war, the venerable Arthur Griffith, the first president of the Free State, died suddenly in August, 1922. In the ensuing power vacuum William Cosgrave took the helm of the Dáil, and though the means by which he brought order back to Ireland often left him a minority in the Dáil, he faced little opposition. The terms of the Anglo-Irish Treaty (passed in January 1922) required an oath of allegiance to the British crown, among other insults. Refusing to take the oath meant that Republican factions could not participate in parliamentary affairs. Few industrialized spots on the globe escaped the economic depression of the early 1930s, and the Free State was as rife with public discontent as anywhere else. After ten years in power, Cosgrave's administration was defeated by Eamon de Valera's Fionna Fail party, in 1932. Five years later de Valera's constitution passed on national referendum. The new country was called Eire, or Ireland, and measures were taken to cut ties to the government of Great Britain. Article I of the new Irish constitution evokes the spirit of its character from the first:

> The Irish nation hereby affirms its inalienable, indefeasible, and sovereign right to choose its own government, to determine its relations with other nations, and to develop its life, political, economic and cultural, in accordance with its own genius and traditions.

That the Irish, after centuries of oppression, should insist at the earliest opportunity, on their cultural rights by virtue of unique genius and traditions is a testament to the power and place of literature and the success of the Revival. Fittingly, Douglas Hyde, the Celtic scholar, was chosen as Ireland's first president in 1937.

But de Valera's governance came to border on totalitarianism. With the advent of the Second World War, a series of laws held over from the Irish Free State were muffling this "genius" of Irish literature. Ireland pledged neutrality during World War II, and the offices of the Censorship Board, established under the Censorship of Publications Act in 1929, saw to it that all printed media reflected the positions of the Republic. With a hearty bow to the Church, the Act was originally conceived to keep salacious English magazines out of the country, but in time the Censorship Board took to task any influence it deemed corrupting. Special "emergency" restrictions during the war had newspapers censored to ostensible neutrality. The first pictures of the devastation in London were only printed in 1945, after the Allies had won. Books that appeared to endorse any outside influences were banned. The war on words grew feverish during the war and somewhat analogous to McCarthyism in the 1950s, with the board pursuing authors who dared to write against their efforts. Censors were particularly vigilant toward English views in the interest of maintaining Irish identity, though they were not beyond banning books that presented a view of Ireland

The Preamble to the Constitution of Ireland

In the Name of the Most Holy Trinity, from Whom is all authority and to Whom, as our final end, all actions both of men and States must be referred,

We, the people of Éire,
Humbly acknowledging all our obligations to our Divine Lord, Jesus Christ, Who sustained our fathers through centuries of trial,
Gratefully remembering their heroic and unremitting struggle to regain the rightful independence of our Nation,
And seeking to promote the common good, with due observance of Prudence, Justice and Charity, so that the dignity and freedom of the individual may be assured, true social order attained, the unity of our country restored, and concord established with other nations,
Do hereby adopt, enact, and give to ourselves this Constitution.

that was less than gleaming white. This came to a head when the Board banned Eric Cross's *The Tailor and Ansty*, an authentic account of the life and opinions of an old Gougane Barra peasant named Timothy Buckley, on the grounds of indecency. "This is entertaining," wrote author Sean O'Faolain for the *New York Times* soon after the book was banned, because "that means that the censorship has at last come up against the sacrosanct Gaelic Revival" (February 14, 1943). In the course of a fevered campaign against *The Tailor* several clergymen tracked down the tailor himself, forced him to his knees and made him burn copies of the book, resulting in a scandal that saw the ban on *The Tailor* lifted. As is usually the case, *The Tailor and Ansty* was thereafter found to be fairly tame. Most modern editions of the book are introduced by Frank O'Connor, who tells the story of the ban on *The Tailor*.

SEAN O'FAOLAIN

If something like an intellectual monolith developed through the de Valera administration, Sean O'Faolain came to stand in opposition. Baptized John Francis Whelan in 1900, he was born to a staunch Anglophile in Cork, becoming a convert after the display of British justice during the Easter Rising, 1916. In 1918 he enrolled at University College in Cork, and grew his hair long. His new nationalism inspired him to learn Gaelic, change his name, join the Irish Volunteers and later the I.R.A., where, without the taste for bomb-making, he served the organization, at the tender age of twenty-three, as its director of publicity. His coming-of-age, then, coincided with that period of Irish history known as "the Troubles," and the fiction he began to write consisted mainly of provincial stories surrounding Irish freedom fighters. O'Faolain, along with his friend Frank O'Connor, met and became acolytes of the Cork-based author Daniel Corkery. Soon disillusioned with the thoughtless zealotry of too many members of the I.R.A., and angry with Corkery for romanticizing their endeavors in his stories, he determined that Ireland might be served in other, better ways. He found Ireland's artistic introversion and its obsession with peasant culture and poverty too narrow and worse yet, backward-looking. After winning a fellowship to Harvard, he married, taught in America and London, and returned to Ireland in 1933, where he settled in County Wicklow, fifteen miles from Dublin. With a second child on the way, in 1937 the O'Faolains bought an acre of land in Knockaderry, the south Dublin suburb, and built a house with a view of the city. Except for long sojourns in Italy, O'Faolain lived and wrote in Knockaderry until 1972, when he and his wife removed to a house called Rosmeen Park in Dun Laoghaire, not far from Joyce's tower.

Sean O'Faolain wrote four novels and several works of non-fiction in his lifetime, but his reputation rests on his short stories. His first collection, *Midsummer Nights Madness*, was published in 1932 and swiftly banned in Ireland, mostly for a mention of a young girl's 'titties,' but it won him instant and international fame. A *New York Times* reviewer hailed O'Faolain as a master of the form, the best since Joyce and his *Dubliners*. These, and the stories of his next collection, *A Purse of Coppers*, advocate temperance toward zealous nationalism, with characters that choose to live distant from the cause rather than lose their lives to it—even in spirit. The most pessimistic of O'Foalian's fictions in the '30s raise and cannot answer questions about Ireland's future. In the late 1940s, *Teresa, and Other Stories*, his third collection, introduced the humor, human insight, and nostalgia that became the hallmarks of O'Faolain's writing for the rest of his career.

O'Faolain's vision for Ireland materialized within the pages of his magazine *The Bell*. From its inception in 1940, O'Faolain sought innovation for his magazine, its very title chosen for its dissociation from any of the old nationalist symbols. No longer were the Irish struggling for nationhood—the nation had been won, and it was time to decide what this new country was about. "All our symbols have to be created afresh," he wrote in his first editorial, "and the only way to create a living symbol is to take a naked thing and clothe it with new life, new association, new meaning, with all the vigor of the life we live in the Here and Now" (Harmon 127). Dwelling on the past, he thought, could not foster Ireland's development. His concern was the present, and what was needed, first and foremost, was to instruct the reading public on contemporary Irish life. "When Ireland reveals herself truthfully, and fearlessly, she will be in possession of a solid base on which to build a superstructure of thought, but not until then" (132). Thus O'Faolain instructed his contributors to be documenters first and artists second. Articles were exposés. Short stories were simple, real, slices of life. Its poetry steered away from abstraction.

With such empirical methods, *The Bell* came to the censorship debate as a matter of course. To O'Faolain, Irish censorship was a natural side-effect of a nation in-process, one at pains to decide what sort of country it wanted to be. Even though the editor himself had been stifled by the censors—both *Midsummer Night Madness* and his second novel, *Bird Alone* (1936) were banned—in 1941 and 1942 *The Bell* featured articles on both sides of the issue. But when hard evidence surfaced proving that the Censorship Board had an agenda, which many had long suspected, *The Bell* threw its hat into the ring. O'Faolain and Frank O'Connor, who had been connected to *The Bell* from the beginning, wrote to the *Irish Times*, and O'Faolain motioned to the Minister of the Irish Academy of Letters on the crisis. The Protestant MP John Keane led the charge for the reform of the Censorship Board in the Irish Senate, but when he tried to read the offending passages from *The Tailor and Ansty* to show their relative harmlessness, his foes had the record struck lest the transcripts of the House be purchased as pornography. O'Faolain's biographer Maurice Harmon finishes the story of the debacle with a reflection from the author's diary.

> The [Censorship] Board's Chairman, Professor Magennis, would have none of this. He called The Tailor a sex maniac, said his wife was a moron, and accused Keane of taking his arguments from letters by O'Connor and O'Faolain in the

Irish Times. Keane's motion was defeated. "How the hell," O'Faolain asked himself, "can anyone work in a country where the mob creates such an atmosphere of bigoted ignorance?" (Harmon 139)

O'Faolain's best remembered editorial in *The Bell* lambasted what had become of Ireland under the de Valera administration, for which so many had struggled so long to gain. In this atmosphere, there were calls for the removal of the Minister of Defence because soldiers were playing golf and soccer, not 'national games' like hurling. Between two candidates for a job, the Irish-speaking candidate got the position regardless of qualifications. It was seriously suggested that the details of crimes should be kept out of the newspapers, since such things did not happen in Ireland.

> It is plain to see that our generation has lost all sense of its origins. The healthy, generous, humane sweep of feeling that we associate with the traditions of our countryside no longer runs through society or political life. The very history being pumped into our children in the schools and the image of life being offered to them is all alien alike to our nature and to fact. It is a complete fairy-tale—I have examined scores of these books and speak by the book—based on a fanciful Celtophilism of which you will find no living example if you get on your bicycle and wander through the countryside in search of its exponents. The main notion of it is that we have since the dawn of our history been united there in our efforts to eject all foreign ways, peoples, manners, and customs—which is, of course, arrant nonsense, on this fancy there has been piled up a gospel of the sanctity of the West and the evil of the East, the generative power and utter purity of all native custom and tradition, as handed down by an army of, mainly legendary, saints and heroes; a thirst for not only what little remains of this custom and tradition but the revival of what of it is actually dead or obsolescent; a

drive towards authoritarianism to enforce these ideas and a censorship of cold-blooded economic pressure (which we all feel, and which business-men carefully watch) to down everybody who opposes them. This farrago is called Nationalism. (Deane 101)

For O'Faolain, the dependence on a contrived, homogeneous culture based too much on myth had the whole country living a fallacy. The root cause was that nobody had bothered to imagine what to do with the country once it materialized, and de Valera's conservative, isolationist, defensive posture in education and the arts would only, could only, narrow the country's intellectual resources. O'Faolain continued to endorse the same conclusion he came to when he fell out with Corkery: that a myopic definition of Irishness would only create myopic Irishmen; that overdwelling on a defeated Irish past cannot contribute to the Irish future; that Ireland belonged within (and had much to contribute to) European tradition and world literature.

FRANK O'CONNOR

In the conservatism of 1940s Ireland, O'Faolain had few on his side. James Joyce had been predicting some such "paralysis" since the turn of the century, and had left the country for that reason. George Bernard Shaw and Samuel Beckett likewise escaped. Dublin academics shied away from his outspoken magazine. But Frank O'Connor, who met Sean O'Faolain back in the twenties through the I.R.A., lived in this sanctimonious, stagnant Dublin, was himself snubbed by it, and did not hesitate to opine.

Famous today for his short stories (for he, too, occupied that heyday before the advent of television), O'Connor's big break came from Æ, who saw his stories into *The Irish Statesman*. After a bound collection (*Guests of the Nation*, 1931) and a novel (*The Saint and Mary Kate*, 1932), O'Connor became the director of the Abbey Theatre at Yeats's behest. But service in that capacity put him at loggerheads with Irish censorship, and O'Connor was only able to stand three years, from 1936 to 1939, before he was forced out of the position. A novel, *Dutch Interior*, was banned in 1940, as were the short story collections *Crab Apple Jelly* in 1940, *The Common Chord* in 1947, and *Traveller's Samples* in 1951, after which he moved to America. Just before enough was enough, he wrote an essay for the magazine *Holiday* where he spoke of Ireland as it was: "a mess, and one which will take more than my lifetime to clear up, but it can be cleared up and is a job worth the doing" (Steinman 394). As for Dublin, to which he returned before his death, teaching at Trinity, O'Connor recorded genially its reduced state:

> Dublin, where I spend my days, is a beautiful city with the mountains behind it and the sea in front, and what more can a man ask? It has no industries to speak of, except beer and biscuits. It has the worst slums in Europe, which is what happens when you build a great aristocratic capital of hour-story Georgian mansions without the industry to support it. (Families of six and seven people live in one room, with spindly-legged children dragging water up the great ruined staircases from the yard.)
>
> Dublin has three newspapers, none of which publishes any news. It has one good restaurant and a line of good old Joycean hotels like the Dolphin and the Wicklow where the steaks and beer are excellent and the waiters get to know your life story in two evenings. It has two cathedrals, both Protestant, and two universities, one Protestant and one Catholic, but except that the Protestant one, Trinity, has the Book of Kells, there is little to choose between them. Catholics are debarred by their own archbishop from attending Trinity, but they attend just the same—probably they like looking at the Book of Kells. It has two theatres, one, the Gate, where they produce Continental and English plays; the other, the Abbey, where they produce Irish ones, or variety shows in

Gaelic. The pubs are good and the company there is good, for they are filled with distinguished writers you never heard of, since their works have never reached beyond the pubs. (Steinman 394)

In dredging up the writers of the Irish pub scene, O'Connor is certainly thinking of Brian O'Nolan, the Dublin novelist and columnist, who went by many names. Since October 1940 he had become famous in the city under the pseudonym Myles na Gopaleen, whose column *Cruiskeen Lawn* (Irish for 'the little overflowing jug') would appear in the *Irish Times,* with a few interruptions, until his death in 1966. But he is best known to literature as Flann O'Brien, with *At Swim-Two-Birds* his first and most salient novel.

FLANN O'BRIEN

O'Brien was born in Strabane, County Tyrone, in 1912. His was certainly one of the few Irish-speaking households in the area. O'Brien's father had learned Irish through the influence of the Gaelic League and insisted it be spoken at home. Following frequent moves, the family came to Dublin in 1925, living for a few years at 25 Herbert Place near the Grand Canal before settling into their permanent home in Blackrock, at 4 Avoca Terrace. He attended the Christian Brothers School in Synge Street, and in 1929 enrolled at University College, Dublin, where much of *At Swim-Two-Birds* takes place.

After four years O'Brien finished his Master's thesis, "Nature in Irish Poetry," which rethought the bizarre assumptions handed down from the Irish Literary Revival that had the ancient Celt so intoxicated with nature that he seriously entertained notions of, say, turning into a bird. His paper sought to demonstrate that nature had the same, largely aesthetic appeal for the ancient Irish poets as it did for those of any age and culture, and little more. But long on regard for the old literature and short on academic rigor, his thesis was rejected. With special permission he was allowed to revise and resubmit his work, which he finally did—according to one of the most treasured anecdotes of the students at UCD—on pink paper.

On the same pink paper, in an upstairs room at the family home on Avoca Terrace, on a desk he built himself, Brian O'Nolan—or rather, Flann O'Brien—crafted *At Swim-Two-Birds* in 1935. He began that summer while rewriting his thesis, and probably finished the novel before the New Year. He shelved it on completion. O'Brien never expected to publish the book because he was starting, that year, his post in the Irish civil service, which left little room for writing on the side.

Affinity between *At Swim* and O'Brien's master's thesis extends well beyond the color of the paper. As a frame story *At Swim*'s narratives plunge several layers deep, and O'Brien drew some stories from Irish myth, especially the folktales of the giant Finn MacCool and the Middle Irish text *The Madness of Sweeney*, the latter of which figured heavily in his thesis. But with little of the reverence for Gaelic legend possessed by his literary forbears in the Revival, O'Brien subverts the ancient texts to suit his own purposes. The hyperbole in the sections dealing with Finn MacCool is hilarious. The Pooka MacPhillemy, "a member of the devil class" (O'Brien 9), an Irish trickster figure traditionally more evil than mischievous, is courteous and morally upright. Allusions to the Ulster cycle's *Táin Bó Cuailnge* ("The Cattle-Raid of Cooley") have cowboys running a ranch in Dublin. Using Irish literature in this way, O'Brien nods to the past, creates a wholly innovative fiction by it, and at the same time ridicules the idea that it has some place in the modern nation of Ireland.

Today, *Finnegans Wake*, which was also published in 1939 and to which *At Swim* is constantly compared, reads like an anomaly. *At Swim-Two-Birds*, in contrast, is an anachronism. Its characteristics are remarkably similar to those postmodern fictions that arose three decades later. What we have from the author—who wrote under a pseudonym, remember—is the story of a college student, who endeavors to write a novel about an author, Dermot Trellis, engaged in writing a book himself.

Trellis is a slothful man, however, and in the many hours he sleeps each day his characters, regretful of their assigned roles, revolt against their author. Throughout the novel they tell their own stories, and while living lives often the opposite of what Trellis intends, they decide to write their own vengeful story of their creator. With this obvious display of the artifice of the novel, the multiple styles in which *At Swim* is told, the inclusion of texts as varied as American westerns and Irish myth, and the multiple beginnings and endings, *At Swim-Two-Birds* has all the tropes of postmodernism.

When O'Brien set aside the manuscript of *At Swim-Two-Birds* in 1935 it contained lengthier passages dealing with the Gaelic legends than the book published in 1939. His father died in 1937 leaving little to support the large family he left behind, and it fell to O'Brien to provide for his mother and his nine younger siblings. The event forced him to reconsider writing as a supplement to his wages from the civil service. He pared down his book and sent it off. Longman's agreed to publish it on the advice of Graham Greene, then a reader for the firm. It sold miserably—only 244 copies in six months—despite the blessings of James Joyce (practically blind by now, *At Swim* was likely the last book Joyce read) and Dylan Thomas, among others. It was doomed to obscurity when the Longman's warehouse was blown up in the Blitz, and not republished until 1960, recognized thereafter as a masterpiece of Irish literature.

In the meantime, Brian O'Nolan needed cash. He wrote two articles for O'Faolain's *The Bell* in its 1940 inaugural issue under the name Flann O'Brien, attracting the attention of the editor of the *Irish Times*, who, already delighted with some acerbic letters he had written to the paper, offered O'Nolan a column.

Cruiskeen Lawn ran for the better part of twenty-six years, during which time it ran the gamut from funny to fierce, and at its best, both at once. O'Nolan's position in the civil service kept him close to the workings of the Dáil, and combined with his presence in pubs and in literary circles, all Dublin was his to build up or blast. The column was always in Gaelic until 1943, but as the years passed, readers of the *Times* literate in Irish grew fewer, until at last the column became wholly English. Its success landed O'Nolan a book deal almost immediately. On the coattails of his column, Myles na Gopaleen's *An Beal Bocht*, translated since O'Nolan's death as *The Poor Mouth*, outsold two printings. He followed this with a play, *Faustus Kelly*, which ran for two weeks in early 1943, but suffered from the high hopes of *Cruiskeen Lawn*'s readership.

Though O'Nolan had been a drinker since his college days, boredom with his civil service job had him in the Scotch House, at the corner of Burgh Quay and Hawkins Street, before lunch. His drinking from 1943 onward never slackened, and though he kept his job (it was nearly impossible to be fired from the civil service) he accomplished little; his columns suffered, becoming in the 1950s outright hostile; writing fiction was out of the question. By 1954 he had offended too many, and was forced to resign from the civil service. For years, he drank in town all day—at Mulligan's on Poolbeg Street, where Joyce set a scene in his short story "Counterparts"; at the Palace Bar on Fleet Street, where the Dublin literary set did their drinking; or at McDaid's on Harry Street, where he associated with that other notorious Dublin drinker, Brendan Behan. He came home to write his columns in the late afternoon, and was often in bed by evening.

O'Nolan narrowly escaped the lot of Brendan Behan, whose drinking all but ended his career five years before he died of alcohol-induced diabetes. In 1959 he was contacted by a London publisher interested in reissuing *At Swim-Two-Birds*, and it appeared the next year, lauded on both sides of the Atlantic. Two more novels soon followed, *The Hard Life* (1961) and *The Dalkey Archive* (1964), featuring a pious James Joyce working as a barkeep in Skerries, North Dublin, dreaming of a new life as a Jesuit. Elements of the former are almost catcalls at the Irish censors; the main character is a priest named Father Fahrt; and O'Nolan in fact geared up for a legal battle over the book, but the censors did not bite, and the publisher's Dublin supplies were gone in two days. *The Third Policeman*, which he wrote after *At Swim* (but because he was unhappy with it, buried for decades), was published posthumously in 1967. With critical attention, it may someday rival *At Swim-Two-Birds* as Flann O'Brien's masterpiece.

PATRICK KAVANAGH

Though they had occasional spats, the poet Patrick Kavanagh was inevitably close to O'Brien's post-War literary set. He too was not a native Dubliner, born into the Irish peasantry of Inniskeen, County Monoaghan and only landing in Dublin in 1939. "It was the worst mistake of my life," (Kavanagh, *Self-Portrait* 11). He had been writing what he knew of the Irish peasantry, but was compelled, once in Dublin, to adhere to the conventions of the Irish literary revival. Thanks to his own familiarity with the life of Ireland's rural poor he came, in time, to see the holdovers of the Revival for their affectation: it was clear that these—the only writers making a living then—knew nothing of peasant life. He wrote *The Great Hunger*, his longest and most famous work for 1942, which centers on a peasant farmer who forsakes his sexual and spiritual happiness to work the thankless land.

> He shook a knowing head
> And pretended to his soul
> That children are tedious in the hurrying fields of April
> Where men are spanging across wide furrows.
> Lost in the passion that never needs a wife—
> The pricks that pricked were the pointed pins of harrows.
> Children scream so loud that the crows could bring
> The seed of an acre away with crow-rude jeers.

The book was banned. A section of the poem appeared in the London periodical *Horizon*, which had the police about Dublin rounding up copies. Incensed that the reading public welcomed the hypocrisy of his contemporaries, through the '40s and '50s he turned to journalism, writing gossip columns, and movie and television reviews. His own newspaper, *Kavanagh's Weekly*, began in 1952 but folded after thirteen issues.

On June 16, 1954, Kavanagh was one of a small group celebrating the first Bloomsday, fifty years from Joyce's first date with Nora Barnacle. As Bloomsdays go, their odyssey was rather abortive; Flann O'Brien was already drunk when they set off that morning from the Martello Tower, and the rest of the party, including John Ryan, editor of the literary magazine *Envoy* (whose idea it was in the first place), Anthony Cronin, later O'Brien's biographer, and Tom Joyce, cousin to James, caught up with O'Brien by the afternoon. Too soggy by then to continue north of the Liffey into nighttown, they ended in John Ryan's pub, the Bailey, on Duke Street. Ryan later had the foresight to rescue the door of 7 Eccles Street from demolition, taking it to the Bailey, where, in a small ceremony, Patrick Kavanagh declared it 'shut.' There the door was on display for many years, until it became a permanent exhibit at the James Joyce Centre. A recent remodeling has left the Bailey with no reminders of the days when it housed Dublin's literary throng, though each night at 7:30 (four days a week in the winter months) the Dublin Literary Pub Crawl begins here. A tour of the Dublin haunts of the city's most famous writers, sojourners on the Crawl meet actors playing the likes of Yeats, Behan, Joyce, Wilde, Beckett, O'Casey, Stephens, and many others.

In the summer of 1955, along the bank of Dublin's Grand Canal, Kavanagh was convalescing from recent surgery when he found a new muse. He later termed it a "poetic hegira," where, rejecting his previous work, he gave up his quest for literary greatness, and would thereafter write with a certain passivity, taking stock in the sensations around him without regard for a purpose. In "Canal Bank Walk" (1960), he set his epiphany in verse, beseeching the world to "Feed the gaping need of my senses, give me ad lib / To pray unselfconsciously with overflowing speech" (lines 11–12). Allowing the words to do their own work, Kavanagh had at last found peace.

Leafy-with-love banks and the green waters of the canal
Pouring redemption for me, that I do
The will of God, wallow in the habitual, the banal,
Grow with nature again as before I grew.
("Canal Bank Walk")

Kavanagh married for the first time in 1967, and died later that year. He is remembered today in Dublin as he wished, with a bench along the banks of the Grand Canal. Inscribed on "the bench with the stench," as the Dublin wits have it, are Kavanagh's own words:

O commemorate me where there is water,
Canal water preferably, so stilly
Greeny at the heart of summer. Brother
Commemorate me thus beautifully.
Where by a lock Niagariously roars
    The falls for those who sit in the tremendous silence
Of mid-July. No one will speak in prose
    Who finds his way to these Parnassian islands.
A swan goes by head low with many apologies,
Fantastic light looks through the eyes of bridges—
    And look! a barge comes bringing from Athy
And other far-flung towns mythologies.
O commemorate me with no hero-courageous
Tomb—just a canal-bank seat for the passer-by.
    ("Lines Written on a Seat on the Grand Canal, Dublin")

CONTINUING DUBLIN'S LEGACY

These days, Dublin continues to produce some of the best of the world's literature in English. Since the deaths of Sean O'Faolain and Samuel Beckett, whose long lives extended well into the modern era, a number of Dublin authors have made permanent inroads in contemporary literature. William Trevor, who read history at Trinity College, is the clear inheritor to the legacy of James Joyce. His hundreds of short stories, while often comical, lend insight into the underbelly of humanity, with alienated souls agonizing against the limitations of society.

More than any other living poet, Thomas Kinsella has embraced Dublin as his subject. His early "Baggot Street Deserta" has the speaker isolated from the city, working late in the attic of his Baggot Street house. Alone with his art he can only imagine the real world outside, but rather than despair of the artist's distance from his subject, there is, in the end, a connection to the outside, however minor it may seem:

> Out where the imagination arches
> Chilly points of light transact
> The business of the border-marches
> Of the Real, and I—a fact
> That may be countered or may not—
> Find their privacy complete.
>
> My quarter-inch of cigarette
> Goes flaring down to Baggot Street.

Kinsella lived in the city until the mid-sixties, when he began taking teaching jobs in America, first at Southern Illinois University, and later at Temple in Philadelphia. "Phoenix Park," in his 1967 collection *Nightwalker*, remembers Dublin as he prepares to leave the city of his birth. He and his wife travel by car along the Liffey to a bar in Lucan, outside the city, where they both worry at the uncertainty of leaving Dublin:

> To sit in a back bar in Lucan
> At a glass table, under a staring light,
> Talking of departure. You are uneasy;
> I make signs on the surface with my wet glass
> In human regret, but human certainty:
>
> Whatever the ultimate grotesqueries
> They'll have to root in more than this sour present.

The ordeal-cup, set at each turn, so far
We have welcomed, sour or sweet. What matter where
It waits for us next, if we will take and drink?

Like James Joyce and Flann O'Brien, Kinsella managed to honor Ireland's literary heritage without succumbing to the conventions of the Irish literary revival. He paid homage to the *Táin Bó Cuailnge* with a translation in 1969, which stays true to the text without the pretentious embellishment of earlier translations. And *Notes from the Land of the Dead and Other Poems* (1973) marries the earthy Celtic veneration of nature with Kinsella's experimental style and self-reflexivity. He retired in 1990, and is now living in County Wicklow.

Eavan Boland has nine collections of poetry, and lives in the Dublin suburb of Dundrum. She too has found a place for her city in her poems, especially regarding its multicultural disunity which, for Boland, is too important to Dublin's past to pretend, as Yeats did, that some sort of cultural unity is possible. In "Colony," from her 1998 collection *The Lost Land*, even the natural formations underneath Dublin are boundaries and dividing lines:

Here is the city—
its worn-down mountains,
its grass and iron,
its smoky coast
seen from the high roads
on the Wicklow side.
 From Dalkey Island
to the North Wall,
to the blue distance seizing its perimeter,
its old divisions are deep within it.
 And in me also.
And always will be.

But Boland is best known for her feminist poetry, particularly her works dealing with a woman's body and motherhood. "Anna Liffey," from 1994's *In a Time of Violence*, reconciles an aging woman's body, which like the Liffey, is from the beginning on a course to its own dissolution in the ocean, but which is also a source of history and life. Boland's last volume of verse, *Against Love Poetry*, was published in 2001.

Since the 1980's Dermot Bolger, Roddy Doyle, and Maeve Binchy have been the darlings of Dublin fiction. Bolger's first novel, *Night Shift* (1985), introduced readers to industrialized Dublin, with all the trappings of the contemporary metropolis—where under the neon lights of O'Connell Street aimless children sniff glue and beg for money, young girls offer themselves for heroin, skinheads play-fight in the traffic, and half-drunk citizens line up for hamburgers and french fries. Bolger devised and contributed to *Finbar's Hotel*, published in 1997, a series of interrelated short stories all taking place in a quayside Dublin hotel the night before its demolition. Each of the seven chapters was written by a different Dublin author, though they are anonymous, leaving the reader to discern which hand spun which yarn. Enormously popular in Ireland and England, Bolger followed up with *Ladies' Night at the Finbar Hotel* in 1999. Roddy Doyle, a Dublin-born UCD alumnus, won the Booker Prize in 1993 for *Paddy Clark Ha Ha Ha*, an often funny story of Irish adolescence in the late sixties. In this and in the novels of his "Barrytown trilogy," especially *The Commitments*, about the travails of a Dublin soul band, Doyle captures the ring of Dublin slang speech.

With fifteen novels, three collections of short stories, two plays, and a work of nonfiction, Maeve Binchy is easily the most popular of Dublin's contemporary writers. She grew up in Dalkey, attended UCD, and still lives in the south Dublin suburb of her birth. Like Flann O'Brien, Binchy got her start from a letter she wrote to the *Irish Times*, but the similarities end there: it seems unlikely that Oprah's Book Club will recommend *At Swim-Two-Birds* anytime soon.

Perhaps the most promising author from Dublin in recent

memory is Jamie O'Neill, who wrote his 2001 *At Swim, Two Boys* over a period of ten years while working a night job in a London psychiatric hospital. With a gift for prose, the Dun Laoghaire native has written his way into the Irish literary tradition. The title, of course, suggests influence from O'Brien, but Joyce is never very far away—quite literally. In the novel, two boys at the Forty Foot baths, in the shadow of Joyce's tower, agree to swim the next Easter to Muglin's Rock, the small island out in Dublin Bay, where they will make it their own. But in that time, as the tension in Dublin rises, the boys fall in love until the city erupts in armed revolt on Easter Monday, 1916. Linking the warm but taboo relationship between the boys with the event that led directly to the founding of Ireland, O'Neill shows a nation about to change utterly.

The River Liffey divides Dublin into two distinct halves: south of the river, and north of the river.

SOUTH OF THE LIFFEY

DAVY BYRNES PUB

21 Duke Street • Tel: 353 1 677 5217
www.davybyrnespub.com

The pub where Leopold Bloom ate his famous lunch has embraced its place in literature, and visitors might still order up a gorgonzola sandwich, or choose from a selection of Dublin's unique pub food. It is now one of the most fashionable bars in Dublin, just off the shopping district of Grafton Street.

LEINSTER HOUSE

Kildare Street and Merrion Square • Tel: 353 1 618 3036

Home to the Dáil since 1924, this 1745 building was once the headquarters of the Royal Dublin Society, which made it the cultural epicenter of Dublin after 1815. A guided tour can be arranged through the Public Relations office even when the Dáil is in session (Tuesday through Thursday, October through May) with a call ahead of time.

MARSH'S LIBRARY

Staint Patrick's Close and Upper Kevin Street •
Tel: 353 1 454 3511
www.marshlibrary.ie

Founded in 1701 by Narcissus Marsh, the Provost of Trinity College while Jonathan Swift was a student, it is Ireland's oldest public library. Home to a great collection of ancient books, many of which are often exhibited for display, the library was also frequented by the eminent eighteenth century writers William Carleton and Charles Robert Maturin.

THE NATIONAL LIBRARY OF IRELAND

Kildare Street • Tel: 353 1 603 0200
www.nli.ie

In addition to being the primary depository for the manuscripts and personal papers of authors from Maria Edgeworth to Patrick Kavanagh, the Library also holds a wealth of genealogical records, and its National Photographic Archive counts over 300,000 pictures of Irish history.

SAINT PATRICK'S CATHEDRAL

21–50 Patrick's Close • Tel: 353 1 475 4817
www.stpatrickscathedral.ie

Jonathan Swift served as dean in this ancient cathedral for more than thirty years, and he and his beloved Stella are buried here. Visitors are welcomed daily except during Sunday services, when the cathedral is restricted to worshippers.

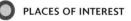

ST. STEPHEN'S GREEN

At the city's center, this 27 acre park was opened to the public in 1880. As the last stand of the Irish Volunteers during the Easter Rising, the park features the bust of the rebel leader Countess Markievicz, in addition to statues of Yeats and Mangan, and a bust of James Joyce.

TRINITY COLLEGE LIBRARY

Tel: 353 1 608 2320

Literary alumni of Trinity College run the gamut from Swift to Beckett. The architecture on campus is breath-taking in its own right, but visitors will want to wander to the Old Library, where two volumes of the priceless Book of Kells are always on display. The Old Library and its famous Long Room are free to visit.

OSCAR WILDE HOUSE AND OSCAR WILDE STATUE

1 North Merrion Square • Tel: 353 1 662 0281
www.amcd.ie/oscarwildehouse/about.html

In 1855 William Wilde, his wife 'Speranza,' and their one-year-old son Oscar moved into the house on 1 North Merrion Square. The family lived in the house up through Oscar's studies at Trinity, and in 1994 the house was taken over by the American College Dublin. Much of the house has been restored to how it likely appeared in Oscar's time. Across the street, reclining on a rock is the Oscar Wilde statue. Sculpted by Danny Osborne and unveiled in 1997, the colorful statue is a lifelike representation of the flamboyant writer.

BIRTHPLACE OF GEORGE BERNARD SHAW

33 Synge Street • Tel: 353 1 872 2077

Shaw's first home, restored to its original Victorian grandeur, is open to the public from May through October. For those seeking a glimpse into life in Victorian Dublin, the house is not to be missed.

NORTH OF THE LIFFEY

THE ABBEY THEATRE

26 Lower Abbey Street • Tel: 353 1 878 7222
www.abbeytheatre.ie

Though the building Yeats knew was destroyed by fire in 1951, the Abbey's new building opened on the same site in 1966. A schedule of upcoming shows is available on the theatre's website.

THE DUBLIN WRITERS MUSEUM

18 Parnell Square North • Tel: 353 1 872 2077

Showcasing an array of the manuscripts and memorabilia from many of Dublin's most famous authors in a spectacular eighteenth century Georgian townhouse, the Museum also features a bookstore and restaurant, and often holds readings and lectures.

THE JAMES JOYCE CENTRE

35 North Great George's Street • Tel: 353 1 878 8547

Joyce enthusiasts need not wait for Bloomsday to walk the streets of Joyce's Dublin. A different guiding walking tour leaves from here at 2 P.M. Tuesday, Thursday, and Saturday. The Centre features a bookshop and rotating exhibhits, and houses the original door to 7 Eccles Street, the home of Leopold Bloom.

OTHER EXCURSIONS

THE DUBLIN LITERARY PUB CRAWL

9 Duke Street • Tel: 353 1 6705602

At 7:30 P.M. nightly from April through November, and on Thursday, Friday, Saturday, and Sunday the rest of the year, the Pub Crawl leaves from the Duke Pub, off Grafton Street. The tour offers a walking guide to some of the most famous literary pubs in Dublin, and along the way attendees are treated to actors in the characters of Dublin's greatest authors, who act out scenes and recite their works.

JAMES JOYCE TOWER

Sandycove • Tel: 353 1 872 2077

Though Joyce only lived here for six days, he immortalized the two hundred-year-old tower in *Ulysses*, the events of which open here. The round room upstairs has been furnished to look as it did during Joyce's brief stay, and the museum downstairs is filled with Joyceana.

CHRONOLOGY

350 B.C.E.   The first Celts emigrate to Ireland.

c. 450 C.E.   Saint Patrick arrives in Ireland.

795   Viking raids begin.

841–842   Vikings winter in Dublin; establish city as a base for further invasions.

1014   Brian Boru routs the Norse at the Battle of Clontarf.

1170   Strongbow takes Dublin with an army raised in Wales. England's King Henry II arrives soon after to secure his sovereignty.

1348–1349   The Black Death.

1366   Statutes of Kilkenny establish English common law, forbid English colonists to intermarry, wear Irish clothes, speak Gaelic, and participate in certain kinds of trade beneficial to the Irish.

1399   Richard II is deposed; English influence is confined to the Pale through the fifteenth century.

1536   A pliant Irish parliament declares King Henry VIII, who had recently broken with Rome, the head of the state church in Ireland.

1565   Sir Henry Sidney institutes the recolonization of Ireland.

1590   The first three books of Edmund Spenser's *The Faerie Queene* are published in London.

1607   The flight of the earls Tyrconnell and Tyrone, symbolically ending the power of Irish nobles.

1641   Catholics rise against Protestants in Ulster.

1649   Cromwell arrives in Dublin to cheers.

1660	Charles II restored to the English throne.
1662	The Smock Alley Theatre, Dublin's first, is founded.
1667	Jonathan Swift born on November 30.
1670	William Congreve born.
1672	Richard Steele born in Dublin.
1685	James II, a Catholic, sits on the English throne.
1690	King William defeats James II at the Battle of the Boyne.
1695	First Penal Laws against Irish Catholics codified.
1700	Jonathan Swift made prebend of Saint Patrick's Cathedral, Dublin.
1709	Sir Richard Steele starts *The Tatler* in London.
1721	Swift begins writing his *Drapier's Letters*.
1726	*Gulliver's Travels* published.
1729	*A Modest Proposal* published; Congreve and Steele die. Edmund Burke born.
1730	Oliver Goldsmith born.
1745	Jonathon Swift dies.
1746	Henry Grattan born.
1751	Richard Brinsley Sheridan born.
1757	Wide Streets Commissioners begin transforming Dublin.
1769	Maria Edgeworth born.
1775	Daniel O'Connell born.
1779	Thomas Moore born.
1780	Sheridan sits in the British House of Commons. Charles Robert Maturin born.
1782	Henry Grattan's Declaration of Rights pass, winning an independent Irish parliament.
1797	Edmund Burke dies; Samuel Lover born.

1798   Theobald Wolfe Tone and the United Irishmen stage rebellion against English rule.

1800   Edgeworth's *Castle Rackrent* published.

1801   Act of Union takes effect; Irish parliament dissolved.

1803   Robert Emmet executed; James Clarence Mangan born.

1806   Charles Lever born.

1808   First series of Moore's *Irish Melodies* published.

1810   Samuel Ferguson born in Belfast.

1814   Joseph Thomas Sheridan Le Fanu and Thomas Davis born.

1816   R.B. Sheridan dies in utter poverty.

1817   Moore's *Lalla Rookh* published.

1818   William Carleton arrives in Dublin.

1820   Maturin's *Melmoth the Wanderer* published.

1828   George Petrie heads the Ordnance Survey.

1829   Daniel O'Connell wins Catholic Emancipation; Charles Robert Maturin dies.

1830   Carleton's *Traits and Stories of the Irish* Peasantry published; John O'Leary born.

1831   Samuel Ferguson founds the *Dublin University Magazine.*

1832   Cholera outbreak.

1841   O'Connell elected Lord Mayor of Dublin.

1842   Lover's *Handy Andy* published; *The Nation*, newspaper of the Young Irelanders, first published.

1845   The Great Famine begins. Thomas Davis dies of scarlet fever.

1847   Carleton's *The Black Prophet* appears mid-Famine. Bram Stoker born.

1848   Young Irelanders agitate for reform.

1849	Maria Edgeworth dies; Mangan dies.
1852	George Moore born.
1854	Oscar Wilde born.
1856	George Bernard Shaw born.
1863	Le Fanu buys the *Dublin University Magazine*, in which he publishes most of his novels.
1865	William Butler Yeats born.
1867	Fenians rise, quickly put down by English; George Russell (Æ) born in County Armagh.
1869	William Carleton dies; Gladstone disestablishes the Church of Ireland.
1871	John Millington Synge born.
1873	Le Fanu dies; The Home Rule League is founded.
1877	Charles Parnell assumes leadership of the Irish in Parliament.
1879	The Land League is founded.
1880	James Stephens is likely born, though he would claim to share a birthday with James Joyce.
1882	James Joyce born on February 2.
1884	Russell and Yeats meet at the Metropolitan School of Art.
1885	Yeats's career begins.
1886	Sir Samuel Ferguson dies.
1888	George Russell becomes Æ.
1891	Parnell dies.
1894	*Æ's Homeward: Songs by the Way.*
1895	Oscar Wilde's *The Importance of Being Earnest.*
1899	Irish National Theatre stages its first plays.
1900	Oscar Wilde dies; Sean O'Faolain born in Cork.
1902	*Deirdre and Cathleen ni Houlihan* first performed, ensuring the future success of the Irish National Theatre.

1903	Frank O'Connor born Michael O'Donovan in Cork.
1904	James Joyce leaves for Europe.
1905	Æ edits the *Irish Homestead.*
1907	Riots ensue after the performance of Synge's *The Playboy of the Western World.*
1909	J.M. Synge dies.
1911	Moore's *Hail and Farewell* published.
1912	Flann O'Brien (Myles na Gopaleen) born Brian O'Nolan in County Tyrone; James Stephens publishes *The Crock of Gold.*
1914	Joyce's *Dubliners* finally published.
1916	Joyce's *A Portrait of the Artist as a Young Man* published; April: the Easter Rising.
1919	Dáil Éireann forms.
1922	Sylvia Beach publishes *Ulysses* in Paris.
1923	W. B. Yeats wins the Nobel Prize for literature; the Irish Free State is admitted to the League of Nations; Æ founds the Irish Statesman.
1926	Riots after O'Casey's *The Plough and the Stars.*
1928	Thomas Kinsella and William Trevor born.
1929	The Censorship of Publications Act passed.
1932	Eamon de Valera becomes Prime Minister; O'Faolain's *Midsummer Night Madness* (banned).
1935	Æ dies.
1936	Frank O'Connor becomes director of the Abbey Theatre.
1937	The new Constitution of Ireland is passed.
1939	Death of W.B. Yeats; *At Swim-Two-Birds* and *Finnegans Wake* published; Patrick Kavanagh arrives in Dublin.
1940	Sean O'Faolain founds *The Bell*; October: Myles na Gopaleen's *Cruiskeen Lawn* first appears in the Irish Times. Maeve Binchy born.

1941	James Joyce dies in Zürich on January 13.
1942	Patrick Kavanagh's *The Great Hunger* (banned).
1944	Eavan Boland born.
1950	G.B. Shaw and James Stephens die.
1951	The Abbey Theatre burns during a performance of Sean O'Casey's *The Plough and the Stars*.
1952	Beckett's *Waiting for Godot*.
1954	On June 16, the first Bloomsday is marked by Flann O'Brien, Patrick Kavanagh, and others, fifty years from the setting of *Ulysses*.
1956	Kinsella's *Poems*.
1960	*At Swim-Two-Birds* reissued to critical acclaim.
1966	Flann O'Brien (Brian O'Nolan) dies.
1967	Patrick Kavanagh marries and dies; William Trevor's first short story collection, *The Day We Got Drunk on Cake and Other Stories*, is published.
1969	Thomas Kinsella's translation of the *Táin Bó Cuailnge* published; Samuel Beckett wins the Nobel Prize.
1985	Dermot Bolger's *Night Shift*.
1989	Samuel Beckett dies.
1991	Sean O'Faolain dies.
1993	Roddy Doyle's *Paddy Clark Ha Ha Ha* wins the Booker Prize.
1995	Seamus Heaney wins the Nobel Prize.
1996	Eavan Boland's *Collected Poems 1967–1987*.
1997	Finbar's *Hotel* penned by an all-Dublin group of writers.
1998	Eavan Boland's *The Lost Land*.
2001	Boland's *Against Love Poems*.

BIBLIOGRAPHY

Aikin, John. *General Biography; or Lives, Critical and Historical, of the Most Eminent Persons of All Ages, Countries, Conditions, and Professions, Arranged According to Alphabetical Order. Chiefly Composed by John Aikin, M.D. And the Late Rev. William Enfield, LL.D. ...* [Online]. Gale Group, 6/1/2003 1799-1815 [cited 12/24 2004].

Boland, Eavan. *In a Time of Violence.* New York: W.W. Norton & Company, 1994.

———. *The Lost Land: Poems.* New York: W.W. Norton, 1998.

Bolger, Dermot. *Night Shift.* Dingle, Co. Kerry: Brandon, 1985.

Bolger, Dermot et al. *Finbar's Hotel.* London: Picador, 1997.

Burke, Edmund. *A Letter from a Distinguished English Commoner, to a Peer in Ireland, on the Repeal of a Part of the Penal Laws against the Irish Catholics* [Online]. Gale Group, 10/1/2003 1785 [cited 12/28 2004].

———. *The Beauties of the Late Right Hon. Edmund Burke, Selected from the Writings &C. Of That Extraordinary Man, ... To Which Is Prefixed, a Sketch ...* [Online]. Gale Group, 6/1/2004 1798 [cited 12/29 2004].

Byron, George Gordon Byron, Baron. *"Alas! The Love of Women" : 1813-1814.* Edited by Leslie A. Marchand. Vol. 3, *Byron's Letters and Journals.* Cambridge, Mass.: Belknap Press of Harvard University Press, 1974.

Cahill, Susan. *A Literary Guide to Ireland.* Dublin: Wolfhound Press, 1979.

Carleton, William. *The Black Prophet: A Tale of Irish Famine.* Belfast: Simms and M'Intyre, 1847.

———. *The Autobiography of William Carleton.* London: MacGibbon & Kee, 1968.

Carleton, William. *Stories from Carleton, Camelot Series.* New York: W.J. Gage and Co., [1889].

———. *Traits and Stories of the Irish Peasantry.* 4 vols, *Short Story Index Reprint Series.* Freeport, NY: Books for Libraries Press, 1971.

Churchill, Winston. *A History of the English-Speaking Peoples.* 1st ed. 4 vols. Vol. 3. New York: Dodd, Mead, 1956–1958.

Clifford, Brendan. *The Dubliner: The Lives, Times & Writings of James Clarence Mangan.* Belfast: Athol Books, 1988.

Costello, Peter. *Flann O'Brien: An Illustrated Biography.* London: Bloomsbury Publishing, Ltd., 1987.

Davis, Thomas. *Thomas Davis: Selections from His Prose and Poetry.* London; Dublin: Gresham Publishing Co., 1891.

Deane, Seamus, ed. *The Field Day Anthology of Irish Writing.* Vol. 3. New York: W.W. Norton, 1991.

Doyle, Roddy. *The Commitments.* 1st Vintage contemporaries ed. New York: Vintage Books, 1987.

———. *Paddy Clark, Ha Ha Ha.* 1st American ed. New York: Viking, 1994.

Duffy, Charles Gavan. *Young Ireland : A Fragment of Irish History, 1840–1845.* Dublin: M.H. Gill, 1884.

Eagleton, Terry. *Scholars & Rebels in Nineteenth-Century Ireland.* Oxford; Malden, MA: Blackwell Publishers, 1999.

Edgeworth, Richard. *The Substance of Three Speeches, Delivered in the House of Commons of Ireland, February 6, March 4, and March 21, 1800, Upon the Subject of an Union with Great Britain.* [Online]. Gale Group, 10/01/2003 1800 [cited 1/19/2005 2005].

Edgeworth, Maria. *The Absentee.* New York: Penguin Books, 1999.

Egan, Maurice Francis. "On Irish Novels." *Catholic University Bulletin* 10, no. 3 (1904): 329–341.

Foster, R.F., ed. *The Oxford Illustrated History of Ireland.* Oxford; New York: Oxford University Press, 1989.

Goldsmith, Oliver. *The Complete Poetical Works of Oliver Goldsmith.* New York: H. Frowde, 1906.

Gunn, Ian and Clive Hart with Harald Beck. *James Joyce's Dublin : A Topographical Guide to the Dublin of Ulysses: With 121 Illustrations.* New York: Thames & Hudson, 2004.

Hare, Augustus John Cuthbert, ed. *The Life and Letters of Maria Edgeworth.* 2 vols. London: Arnold, 1894.

Harmon, Maurice. *Sean O'Faolain.* London: Constable and Company Limited, 1994.

Hoagland, Kathleen, ed. *1000 Years of Irish Poetry.* New York: Grosset & Dunlap, 1947.

Igoe, Vivien. *James Joyce's Dublin Houses and Nora Barnacle's Galway.* Dublin: Wolfhound Press, 1997.

Irving, Washington. *Oliver Goldsmith : A Biography.* Edited by H.E. Coblentz, *Heath's English Classics.* Boston: D.C. Heath & Co., 1904.

Joyce, James. *A Portrait of the Artist as a Young Man.* New York: Penguin Books, 1916. Reprint, Viking Compass Edition.

———. *Selected Letters of James Joyce.* New York: The Viking Press, 1975.

———. *Ulysses: The Corrected Text.* The Gabler Edition ed. New York: Random House, Inc., 1986.

———. *Dubliners.* New York: Penguin Books, 1996.

Joyce, Stanislaus. *My Brother's Keeper.* New York: The Viking Press, 1958.

Kain, Richard M. *George Russell (A. E.), Irish Writers Series.* Lewisburg, PA: Bucknell University Press, 1976.

Kavanagh, Patrick. *Self-Portrait.* Dublin: Dolmen Press, 1964.

———. *Collected Poems.* New York: Allen Lane, 2004.

Kenny, Herbert. *Literary Dublin: A History.* New York: Taplinger Publishing Company, 1974.

Kiely, Benedict. *Poor Scholar*. New York: Sheed & Ward, 1948.

Kinsella, Thomas. *Collected Poems, 1956–1994*. Oxford; New York: Oxford University Press, 1996.

Le Fanu, Joseph Sheridan. *The House by the Church-Yard, Doughty Library*. London: Blond, 1968.

Lehane, Brendan. *The Companion Guide to Ireland*. Bury St. Edmunds, Suffolk: St. Edmundsbury Press Ltd., 2001.

Lover, Samuel. *Handy Andy, Novels and Tales of Samuel Lover*. University Press of the Pacific, 2001.

Madden, Daniel Owen, ed. *The Speeches of the Right Hon. Henry Grattan: To Which Is Added His Letter on the Union. With a Commentary on His Career and Character*. Dublin: J. Duffy, 1867.

Mangan, James Clarence. *Autobiography*. Edited by James Kilroy, *New Dolmen Chapbooks*. Dublin: Dolmen Press, 1968.

Marsh, Narcissus. *Scholar Bishop: The Recollections and Diary of Narcissus Marsh, 1638–1696*. Cork: Cork University Press, 2003.

Marx, Karl and Friederich Engels, ed. *Marx, Engels on Literature and Art*. Moscow: Progress Publishers, 1976.

Maturin, Charles Robert. *Women; or, Pour Et Contre*. London: Longman, Hurst, Rees, Orme and Brown, 1818.

———. *Melmoth the Wanderer: A Tale*. 4 vols. Vol. 1. Edinburgh: A. Constable and company, 1820.

Mercier, Vivian. *Modern Irish Literature : Sources and Founders*. Edited by Eilís Dillon. Oxford; New York: Claredon Press; Oxford University Press, 1994.

Moore, Thomas. *Tom Moore's Diary*. Edited by J.B. Priestley. Cambridge: Cambridge University Press, 1925.

Mulvey, Helen F. *Thomas Davis and Ireland: A Biographical Study*. Washington, D.C.: Catholic University of America Press, 2003.

O'Brien, Flann. *At Swim-Two-Birds*. 1st Dalkey Archive edition, 1998 ed. Normal, Illinois: Dalkey Archive Press, 1966.

O'Neill, Jamie. *At Swim, Two Boys*. New York: Scribner, 2001.

Piozzi, Hester Lynch. *Anecdotes of the Late Samuel Johnson, LL.D.* Vol. 18, *Johnsoniana*. New York: Garland Publishers, 1974.

Putzel, Steven. "James Stephen's Paradoxical Dublin." In *The Irish Writer and the City*, edited by Maurice Harmon, 103–114. Gerrards Cross, Buckinghamshire: Colin Smythe Limited, 1984.

Russell, Geaorge William. *Letters from A.E.* London; New York: Abelard-Schuman, 1961.

Steinman, Michael, ed. *A Frank O'Connor Reader.* Syracuse, NY: Syracuse University Press, 1994.

Stephens, James. *The Insurrection in Dublin.* New York: The Macmillan Company, 1916.

———. *The Crock of Gold.* New York: The Macmillan Company, 1926.

———. *Collected Poems.* New York: The Macmillan Company, 1954.

Strong, L.A.G. *The Minstrel Boy: A Portrait of Tom Moore.* New York: A.A. Knopf, 1937.

Swift, Jonathan. *Dean Swift's Literary Correspondence, for Twenty-Four Years; from 1714 to 1738. Consisting of Original Letters to and from Mr. Pope, Dr. Swift, ...* Gale, 1741 [cited 12/20/04 2004].

———. *Gulliver's Travels and Other Writings.* Bantam Classic Edition ed. New York: Bantam Books, 1962.

———. *A True Copy of the Late Rev. Dr. Jonathan Swift's Will. Taken from, and Compar'd with, the Original* [Online]. Gale Group, 6/1/2003 [1746] [cited 1/10/05 2005].

Trevor, William. *The Stories of William Trevor.* New York: Penguin Books, 1983.

———. *A Writer's Ireland: Landscape in Literature.* London: Thames and Hudson, 1984.

Yeats, W. B. *Essays and Introductions.* New York: Macmillan, 1961.

———. *Uncollected Prose.* Edited by John P. Frayne. 2 vols. Vol. 1. New York: Columbia University Press, 1970-1976.

———. *The Poems.* New ed. New York: Macmillan, 1983.

Yeats, William Butler. *Autobiographies.* Edited by Richard J. Finneran and George Mills Harper. 12 vols. Vol. 3, *The Collected Works of W.B. Yeats.* New York: Macmillan, 1989.

Cahill, Susan. *A Literary Guide to Ireland*. Dublin: Wolfhound Press, 1979.

Carleton, William. *The Black Prophet: A Tale of Irish Famine*. Belfast: Simms and M'Intyre, 1847.

———. *The Autobiography of William Carleton*. London: MacGibbon & Kee, 1968.

———. *Stories from Carleton, Camelot Series*. New York: W.J. Gage and Co., 1889.

Churchill, Winston. *A History of the English-Speaking Peoples*. 1st ed. 4 vols. Vol. 3. New York: Dodd, Mead, 1956–1958.

Clifford, Brendan. *The Dubliner: The Lives, Times & Writings of James Clarence Mangan*. Belfast: Athol Books, 1988.

Duffy, Charles Gavan. *Young Ireland : A Fragment of Irish History, 1840–1845*. Dublin: M.H. Gill, 1884.

Eagleton, Terry. *Scholars & Rebels in Nineteenth-Century Ireland*. Oxford; Malden, Mass.: Blackwell Publishers, 1999.

Egan, Maurice Francis. "On Irish Novels." *Catholic University Bulletin* 10, no. 3 (1904): 329–41.

Hare, Augustus, John Cuthbert, ed. *The Life and Letters of Maria Edgeworth*. 2 vols. London: Arnold, 1894.

Harmon, Maurice. *Sean O'Faolain*. London: Constable and Company Limited, 1994.

Irving, Washington. *Oliver Goldsmith : A Biography*. Edited by H.E. Coblentz, *Heath's English Classics*. Boston: D.C. Heath & Co., 1904.

Joyce, James. *Ulysses: The Corrected Text*. The Gabler Edition ed. New York: Random House, Inc., 1986.

————. *Dubliners.* New York: Penguin Books, 1996.

Joyce, Stanislaus. *My Brother's Keeper.* New York: The Viking Press, 1958.

Kain, Richard M. *George Russell (A.E.), Irish Writers Series.* Lewisburg, PA: Bucknell University Press, 1976.

Mercier, Vivian. *Modern Irish Literature : Sources and Founders.* Edited by Eilís Dillon. Oxford; New York: Claredon Press; Oxford University Press, 1994.

Mulvey, Helen F. *Thomas Davis and Ireland: A Biographical Study.* Washington, D.C.: Catholic University of America Press, 2003.

Piozzi, Hester Lynch. *Anecdotes of the Late Samuel Johnson, LL.D.* Vol. 18, *Johnsoniana.* New York: Garland Pub., 1974.

Stephens, James. *The Insurrection in Dublin.* New York: The Macmillan Company, 1916.

Strong, L.A.G. *The Minstrel Boy: A Portrait of Tom Moore.* New York: A.A. Knopf, 1937.

WEBSITES

Dublin Writers Museum
www.writersmuseum.com

Irish Writers Centre
www.writerscentre.ie

The James Joyce Centre
www.jamesjoyce.ie/home/

Literary Dublin – Dublin's famous authors, poets, and playwrights
www.dublintourist.com/literary_dublin/

PICTURE **CREDITS**

CONTRIBUTORS

HAROLD BLOOM is Sterling Professor of the Humanities at Yale University. He is the author of over 20 books, including *Shelley's Mythmaking* (1959), *The Visionary Company* (1961), *Blake's Apocalypse* (1963), *Yeats* (1970), *A Map of Misreading* (1975), *Kabbalah and Criticism* (1975), *Agon: Toward a Theory of Revisionism* (1982), *The American Religion* (1992), *The Western Canon* (1994), and *Omens of Millennium: The Gnosis of Angels, Dreams, and Resurrection* (1996). *The Anxiety of Influence* (1973) sets forth Professor Bloom's provocative theory of the literary relationships between the great writers and their predecessors. His most recent books include *Shakespeare: The Invention of the Human* (1998), a 1998 National Book Award finalist, *How to Read and Why* (2000), *Genius: A Mosaic of One Hundred Exemplary Creative Minds* (2002), *Hamlet: Poem Unlimited* (2003), and *Where Shall Wisdom be Found?* (2004). In 1999, Professor Bloom received the prestigious American Academy of Arts and Letters Gold Medal for Criticism, and in 2002 he received the Catalonia International Prize.

JOHN TOMEDI is a freelance writer and researcher living in Howard, Pennsylvania. His previous works include *Kurt Vonnegut* (GREAT WRITERS) and *London*, another title in the BLOOM'S LITERARY PLACES series.